WOMEN MOVING
FORWARD®

WOMEN MOVING
FORWARD®

Over the Years

SUSAN BASH VAN VLEET

Archway Publishing books may be ordered through booksellers or by contacting:

Archway Publishing
1663 Liberty Drive
Bloomington, IN 47403
www.archwaypublishing.com
1 (888) 242-5904

Because of the dynamic nature of the Internet, any web addresses or
links contained in this book may have changed since publication and
may no longer be valid. The views expressed in this work are solely those
of the author and do not necessarily reflect the views of the publisher,
and the publisher hereby disclaims any responsibility for them.

Any people depicted in stock imagery provided by Thinkstock are
models, and such images are being used for illustrative purposes only.
Certain stock imagery © Thinkstock.

ISBN: 978-1-4808-2870-4 (sc)
ISBN: 978-1-4808-2871-1 (e)

Library of Congress Control Number: 2016935189

Print information available on the last page.

Archway Publishing rev. date: 8/5/2016

"I received the gift of being referred to WMF early in my career and have benefited from learning and applying the course concepts for the past 20+ years. If you are ready to stop making excuses, understand what you want to accomplish and put a plan in place to overcome what is getting in your way, it is time to roll up your sleeves and sign up for this terrific training. It has the power to change your life as well as the lives of those who you come in contact with...."

Kate Johnson, President
Gracecamp Consulting
Kate@gracecampllc.com

We are all able to navigate around and avoid the obvious obstacles in our lives. But what about the things we can't see? Or the things of which we are unaware? Women Moving Forward helped me to understand and appreciate myself by removing barriers that I did not know existed. Susan is one of the most insightful, clear, and self-actualized women I have had the opportunity to meet. Her unique blend of candor and insight helped me to be truly aware of myself, my needs, what really goes on around me or _choices that I make_ that rob me of my power and peace of mind. The result? Freedom. I recommend this program without reservation. Susan is changing the world for the better, one woman at a time.

I continue to grow and change for the better years after Women Moving Forward. Apparently, once the flower is encouraged to bloom, it cannot return to being a "bud".

With love and affection,
Diane

"Women Moving Forward® and the Women's Leadership Retreat© have been life changing for me! I wouldn't have the life I have and love today if it weren't for Susan and these workshops!"

"There are so many situations in my life when I can hear Susan's voice saying, 'There just hopping' or 'You need to get over your feeling of powerlessness'; I immediately get back on the right track."

Robin Elston
President
RElston@ElstonConsulting.com
Elston Consulting, LLC

I am only a very recent graduate of WMF (September '08), but what a fabulous experience. My only wish was that I had done it 20 years ago! A colleague who had been on WMF described it as a "gift from the company", which intrigued me and was the final decider in joining. As a Brit we are not so good at the more "touchy/feely" stuff, so was very nervous about going. However I was truly liberated by the experience of WMF, at last realising that I was the only person stopping me from anything I choose to do. The joy and strength I gained from being with a group of women was fantastic and it has really made me appreciate not only my long standing female friends but also how wonderful it is to make new ones. Susan – thank you, thank you and may there be another 30 years!!

Kind regards
Polly

The Women Moving Forward course and learning sharpens your self awareness and explore to be better person in life!

Phoebe Wang, P&G China

-WMF profoundly and permanently affected my life more than any other class or workshop I've experienced.

-Quite simply, it works. You'll know what to do to get 'unstuck.'

-You can't believe the impact just 3 days will have!

-WMF and Susan VV opened my eyes and changed my life. My work and my personal life are forever impacted by the insights and tools from the workshop.

-After WMF, I have a clearer view of myself, the environment around me and how I react. I'm better equipped to stay focused on what matters, leading to improved productivity & effectiveness in all parts of my life.

-Highly recommended for anyone who wants to live with purpose and awareness.

-Come learn how to live on purpose. Your work and life will be better, and the world needs you on purpose.

Chris Nassivera, P&G Boston

I recall the retreat being quite impactful as I had recently completed rounds of chemotherapy and radiation to treat breast cancer. Going through an experience like that, as you might expect, can be quite traumatic, and I found the Leadership Retreat to be an enabler for getting re-grounded post treatment. In other words, it helped to ease back into more of a "normal" professional and personal circumstance while not losing sight of the important lessons I learned during that time. As you teach "living on purpose" as a key element for achieving personal and professional goals as part of the WLR I was able to see how to refocus much of the emotion/energy spent on my treatment experience into more purposeful vein.

Jill Boughton, President & CEO, Sustainable
Waste Resources International

Speaking on behalf of Robin as well, I can tell you this was probably one of the most powerful and effective trainings we've ever attended. The premise of this specific workshop was to help the individual identify the barriers preventing you from achieving your best possible professional performance and then develop strategies and techniques for breaking down these barriers allowing you to be the best leader you can be. These barriers are both internally created, but also external barriers. This particular workshop is very introspective (almost therapeutic) and to be honest, it drums up as many personal issues and development needs as it does professional issues and development needs. The idea is, we each have varying experiences (both positive and negative) that have influenced who we are, how we handle situations, and how we communicate and interact with colleagues on a daily basis. Often, the negative experiences you may have had in your life create obstacles (unconsciously and often self-imposed) for your continued development. Somehow Susan is able to ask the right questions allowing you to identify these barriers when you may not have ever connected the dots yourself. After getting to that point (by end of Day 2) she then has you work through exercises that creates a cognizance, goals, objectives, further obstacles, and remedies for those obstacles, and she requires you to identify a timeline to address each. By the nature of what is discovered in Days 1 and 2, these generally aren't simple goals you can achieve in a matter of months or even a year, but rather these are bigger, more strategic goals for personal and professional development. I plan to discuss mine with Mark in my next MAPP meeting.

Nicole McGrath, Assistant Comptroller, Steelcase

The combination of having a room full of amazing successful women with such a mixture of experiences and stories to share and a structure to understand how to achieve your purpose in life makes this course terrific.

Sumaira Latif, IT UK

"The Women Moving Forward® course offered by Susan Van Vleet Consultants, Inc. was such a unique experience and journey that really helped me unlock my true self and understand what had been holding me back in my career and my life. This course helped me identify how I can take charge of my whole life and self and live more fully I highly recommend this course for anyone looking to discover their true potential!"

Cynthia Herrera SCJ Sales

Women Moving Forward is the best thing that happened to me in the area of personal training. It gave me the ability to proactively enhance the relationship with myself (=self confidence) and with my company. This ability makes me a better manager and a better person in life as well.

Linda Bus-Jacobs
PE Manager
Process Excellence & Transformation

"WMF is a life changing experience for women that given some internal and external barriers can't develop themselves to their full potential. WMF has enabled me to be a better mentor and help other women identify some attitudes/beliefs that we not helping them grow and develop to the next level".

Regards,
Claudia Herreramoro
Mexico

WMF changed the entire trajectory of my life. I stopped living the life I thought I was expected to live and started living a life I'd only dreamed was possible.

Hilary Beard
New York Times Best Seller Author

Contents

Acknowledgments

I want to thank the many graduates of the workshop for their undying loyalty to the program and its benefits. Many have sent co-workers and family members to the workshop. If it wasn't for them, it would have died a natural death a long time ago.

I also want to thank John Van Vleet, my husband. We got married the year I created the workshop, and he has been one of its biggest supporters in the almost forty years of the workshop's existence.

Thanks to Charlie and Adam Van Vleet, now thirty-five and thirty, respectively, who, many times a year gave up their mom and her attention to a group of women who will always be grateful to them for their sacrifice.

Thanks to all of the women who taught me how to be a woman and fulfill my destiny, most especially:

Thanks to my mom, Marion Bash, who, even though she could not understand my path, tried hard not to get in my way. I still remember when she proudly put on one of our Women Moving Forward ® t-shirts to sell them to participants when she had just had a mastectomy and wouldn't put on a bathing suit.

Thanks to Grandma Jennie, who was one of the most powerful women I ever knew and who took me under her wing and taught me how and when to use my own power.

Thanks to Grandma Annie for teaching me the power of love and for the gift of security she gave me whenever I was with her. She loved me unconditionally, and that's where I learned how to do that with my children.

Thanks to Preva Cohen, my Hebrew school teacher, who was a rabbi's wife and a rabbi's daughter and made sure I knew how to read from the Torah, pray, and lead a service, even though I was a woman.

Thanks to Mrs. Ida Alphin, my nursery school teacher and later a mentor when I became a first-year social worker at the Division of Youth and Family Services in New Jersey.

Thanks to Gene Weltfish, head of Anthropology at Fairleigh Dickinson Madison, who was my mentor in college and taught me so well about culture and its limitations and gifts.

Thanks to Lorrie Tietze who is also a certified Women Moving Forward ® trainer, for her willingness to take this on and do a fabulous job at it.

Thanks to Leisha Kiel, who I met when our two sons played football together at a Denver prep school and who became my assistant nineteen years ago and since then has been my support in every Women Moving Forward ® workshop I have led.

And, finally, thanks to all the corporate folks, family, and just acquaintances that tried to stop this course and me, those who tried to steal the workshop, those who tried to put me out of business, and those who stood by while others took potshots at the workshop and me. You have taught me so much about perseverance, patience and fearlessness. I owe you a great debt for the lessons I have learned from knowing you.

Enjoy the book!

Susan Bash Van Vleet

President
Susan Van Vleet Consultants ® Inc. and V2 Consulting, Inc.
www.womenmovingforward.com
www.SVanVleetConsult.com
SVVConsult@SVanVleetConsult.com

Introduction

In 1979 I began to develop a course for women that I felt met their needs better than the workshops that were available in the sixties and seventies.

At the time, women were being subjected to workshops like "Dress for Success" and "Assertiveness Training". These programs dealt with the issues women had outside of themselves like dressing well to get a job and communicating in a way the company wanted women to communicate, even if it was a made-up form of communication.

None of the programs at the time dealt with the issues women had on the inside; feeling you are an imposter, having your internal cultural imperatives get in the way of your career, and dealing with a full female life while building a stellar career.

When I developed this program I was sure that when women made it to the top levels of companies they would no longer need the workshop. I was dead wrong. Women need it even more once they make it! The incongruity of their internal and external personas became more acute the more successful they became.

So now, thirty-nine years later, Women Moving Forward® is an international program with women from South America, Central America, North America, Europe (Eastern and Western) and Asia participating either a workshop we have done for their company or in a workshop for the community of companies we set up.

A few years after we began holding Women Moving Forward® workshops, we needed a way to communicate to all of the "graduates" of the course. So we began a quarterly memo that then developed into a monthly newsletter and is now a twice-monthly electronic newsletter called;

The Women Moving Forward® Newsletter, which is sent out to over six hundred Women Moving Forward® graduates in over twenty-five countries.

Welcome to a compilation of these newsletters and it's many articles over the last fifteen to twenty years.

WOMEN MOVING FORWARD®
CHAPTER 1
VIOLENCE AGAINST WOMEN

- Madame Secretary of State Speaks Out on Ending Sexual Violence and Aiding the Victims

- Abuse of Women Increases 42 Percent in the Last Two Years

- More Data on the Increase in Abuse of Women

- The Culture of Silence

- Pedophiles

Madam Secretary of State Speaks Out on Ending Sexual Violence and Aiding the Victims
WMF® Graduates Newsletter, September 2009

Recently. US Secretary of State Hillary Clinton reacted to a misinterpreted question at a press conference. She stated emphatically that she would not give her husband's opinion about an issue and that he was not the Secretary of State: she was!

Although I originally thought the question had been translated incorrectly, which it had not, I have to say I feel for the woman.

I have been the president of a company I started over thirty years ago, before my husband, John, joined the company. Yet in the United States especially, I have been told by potential clients that I'm not really the head of the company, just a figurehead, and there are clients who would like to change our company name to Van Vleet Consultants.

It's interesting that this problem with me being head of my own company occurs mostly in the United States. In Latin America and Asia, I had no problem, and in Europe power is power! But in the good old USA, I still get rude and ridiculous reactions.

However, that's not the real problem here. While the press was focusing on that little vignette, the secretary of state was taking aim at a worldwide problem that is epidemic in the Democratic Republic of Congo and elsewhere: sexual violence against women.

Once again, the US press is more concerned about some gossip than the fact that this is the first time a US secretary of state has gone to Africa and made a public statement against the use of violence toward women as a political tool!

Women are being brutally raped everywhere. In some countries, they are killed to uphold "family honor." As a result of global economic conditions, domestic violence is at epidemic levels, and young women are daily sold into sexual slavery. And for the first time, Hillary Clinton, a US official, addressed this issue.

Finally, we have some government awareness focused on a key issue; and for whatever reason, the press chooses to focus on her retort to an interview question.

I wanted to make sure we gave Secretary Clinton the credit for publicly bringing up the issue of violence against women. Thank you for that! I wanted her to know I heard her, and now you have heard her as well.

It's time we started focusing on this issue worldwide because if the weakest women are abused, then we have not truly broken any glass ceilings! While we've achieved individual accomplishments, our sisters around the world are beaten, raped, and murdered.

And while Hillary is talking to Angolan President Jose Eduardo dos Santos, the rest of us can join groups focused on eradicating violence against women. I belong to one, and many of you do too. Some of you are establishing programs worldwide to combat this real issue.

If you have some experience in the area of preventing violence against women, let us know, and we'll make sure the name of the organization is included in the next newsletter. Then those of you not affiliated with a group actively working on this issue can join one.

Let us know what you think.

Abuse of Women Increases 42
Percent in the Last Two Years
WMF® Graduates Newsletter, January 2010

Shortly before New Year's Eve, I got an e-mail from the executive director of Jewish Women International (www.jwi.org). I support this organization because their mission is to eradicate domestic violence worldwide.

The e-mail had some disturbing new data on the increase of the abuse of women in 2009. A study from the US National Crime Victimization Survey showed a 42percent rise in reported incidents of domestic violence over the past two years, while the overall crime rate has dropped in the United States. The international statistics indicate this increase appears to be present worldwide, although not as large an increase as in the United States. The researchers who conducted the survey postulate that the increase in domestic violence is due, in part, to the difficult economic conditions worldwide.

Historically, women have always been the ones who bear the brunt of the frustration over economic issues. We are always the ones who catch the overflow of anger when things aren't going well economically.

But lately, John and I also have also noticed an increase in institutional abuse of women as well. Institutional abuse is abuse of a class, race, or gender by a company, organization, or government agency. The institution responsible for the abuse can be anything from a corporation who employs women to a nonprofit organization set up to serve women as clients.

In her groundbreaking book *The Addictive Organization*, Anne Wilson Schaef begins the discussion of how organizations themselves can be addictive and therefore abusive. Examples: a female employee has a performance appraisal changed *after* receiving several positive evaluations; an employee is left out of meetings she should be invited to attend; an employee is told she is not a team player or there is something wrong with her attitude, but no one identifies specific behaviors. These are examples of institutional abuse.

A victim of institutional abuse often feels increased stress and lowered self-esteem, similar to victims of domestic violence. However, institutional abuse also produces a general feeling that no one in the organization can be trusted, including good work friends.

Many times, but not always, the human resources department is used as the vehicle through which this abuse is delivered. Sometimes a consulting organization like ours is used. We know some of them. This insidious use of third parties is designed to insulate the organization from appearing to be abusive. Beware of letting yourself or your company be used as insulation.

If you work in human resources and you have been asked to fulfill this abuse, you must state clearly that you will not be a party to this institutional behavior If there is a lawsuit, you may be personally liable.

Here are some suggested responses in case you find yourself in this situation:

1. Find a good attorney, preferably one who has already been successful in opposing the organization abusing you. Get your questions answered, and use the lawyer as a paid sounding board for how to proceed. Sometimes a lawyer

can even give you the precise wording that will communicate clearly to the abusive organization.

2. Make sure your support network outside of work is stronger than your inside network. You need friends whose jobs or personal well being is not threatened when yours is.

   Over the years, friends of mine have told me when they thought nonprofits where I volunteered were abusing me. This feedback helped me to get out of crazy situations so effectively that the abusive organization will never contact me again!

3. Keep your resume updated at all times, and always see a clear path out. Sometimes I feel like a parrot when I speak to women about this issue, but there are some things I can't say often enough.

   You are not being disloyal to your present organization if you interview at another—especially if your present employer is abusive.

   You should always feel as if you can move on and that your current organization doesn't own you. If you feel stuck, and you feel as if you cannot leave, then you are in danger of being a victim—just as a woman in an abusive domestic relationship feels unable to leave.

   Abusive organizations—similar to abusive relationships—can make a woman feel as if their company is the only or the best game in town, and any other organization will be even more abusive. Some companies may use economic conditions to keep abusing an employee—like an abusive spouse controls and tells his or her partner that he or she are nothing without them.

4. Insulate yourself economically. Although this is difficult, especially now, you should always have six to twelve months of salary in savings. If you have a spouse or partner, you should make sure he or she is working and/or are ready to do whatever it takes to support you in removing yourself from the abusive work environment. Research all the information on exit strategies including severance packages. Check with folks who have received packages, and find out how they did it.

But as with any abusive situation, you need to get out safely and quickly, get the exit process started TODAY!

More Data on the Increase in Abuse of Women
WMF® Graduates Newsletter, February 2010

Lori Weinstein, executive director of Jewish Women International, (www.jewishwomeninternational.com) sent the following data regarding international abuse of women. Thank You Lori!

It is estimated that worldwide, one in five women will become a victim of rape or attempted rape in her lifetime. (Referred to by Mara Jos Alcal. State of World Population 2005. *The Promise of Equality: Gender Equity, Reproductive Health and the Millennium Development Goals*. UNFPA. 2005. 65).

In every country where reliable studies have been conducted, statistics show that between 10 percent and 50 percent of women report that they have been physically abused by an intimate partner during their lifetime.

According to the World Health Organization data, the most devastating effect of gender violence worldwide is that violence against women claims almost 1.6 million lives each year—about 3percent of global deaths from all causes.

This is chilling data.

However, I know some of you already are working on this issue; let us know how.

The Culture of Silence
WMF® Graduates Newsletter, June 2010

As you know, many of the women who attend Women Moving Forward® have been abused—physically, emotionally, or sexually during their family life, education, or career. So when I see what is happening to college-age women, I get very upset and look for a way to work toward a world in which young women can attend college without living in fear.

In one incident at a prestigious college, a male varsity lacrosse player allegedly killed his ex-girlfriend, a varsity lacrosse player at the same college.

One of the stunning elements of this story is that there were glaring warning signs of his behavior. Her friends knew he had been physically abusive to her in the past, not to mention his previous arrest record in high school and college.

Why then did they stay silent, and why did they allow this man the time and room to allegedly rape and murder a fellow student on this campus?

He was obviously escalating in his behavior, and yet no one reported him to the university athletic director, the lacrosse coach, or other campus administrators.

What needs to happen to make this violent behavior unacceptable to all who knew about it?

First and foremost, campus policies and procedures must be clear and easy for students to access.

Second, when someone reports a problem or suggests there is a problem, the whole campus needs to respond with a full investigation and legal action.

We are fond of saying that if a company wants to stop sexual harassment, fire one of the perpetrators. That action usually stops similar behavior company wide.

So, if you want to make sure girls in colleges and universities worldwide are safe, start throwing offenders out of the school as unfit to be part of the community. I would be willing to bet the number of incidents would go down just from that action alone.

Third and lastly you must do something about the drug and alcohol abuse at these schools. By all reports the alleged perpetrator in this incident was a "mean drunk", getting into fights every time he got drunk. Just because these kids are almost adults is no excuse for schools to allow this stuff to go on.

I know the Duke University Lacrosse team were innocent of raping the stripper that accused them of rape, but what was going on at Duke that the Lacrosse team had a drunken party with strippers?

If you can give John and I a good explanation for this please let us know.

We can no longer let young women be the fodder for bad policies and out of control young men. If you aren't angry about this, you should be.

Both John and I are angry about this one. Men are just as frustrated about this out of control behavior by the younger versions of themselves as we women are.

I know how John reacted when Charlie & Adam did something he didn't like and I know how that shaped both Charlie and Adam into the men they have become.

If you have feelings about this let us know. We want to hear what you have to say.

Pedophiles
WMF® Graduates Newsletter December 2011

I know this is not a normal holiday topic. But because of all the misconceptions about the Penn State University's retired football coach Jerry Sandusky's actions, I want to shed some light of my own on what is real and imagined and what you can do to protect your children.

I know this scandal has gone International but for those of you who haven't heard, here goes: A retired US University football coach was indicted for allegedly performing acts of pedophilia.

Sandusky was charged with sexually abusing eight (now more) young boys who participated in his "at risk" charity program for young boys. Supposedly he committed forty acts of pedophilia before victims came forward more than twenty years later.

Okay, folks, here's a lesson on pedophiles:

First, they are adults who like to have sex with or fantasize repeatedly about sex with young children.

Second, they can be men or women. The comments that came out after the scandal became public, saying, that if women had been involved the sexual abuse would not have happened were naive at best. I have worked with women pedophiles and they are just as calculating and compulsive as the men.

Third, they have a preference or predilection concerning what they look for. That is, they like ten-to twelve-year old boys and will only go after that category or they like pre-pubescent girls and only go after them. It is rare that they attack children of all ages and genders.

Fourth, they "court" and "seduce" their victims sometimes for years. They have elaborate seductions that usually include tests to see if the child is vulnerable and alone.

Fifth the parents presence and the fear of the parents' involvement with their child is the only thing that will keep your child safe. To predators that means your child is *not* vulnerable and alone. This does not mean you have to be with your child all day everyday. When we suspected people at Charlie's school were pedophiles we made sure they were afraid we would sue them or report them to the police and social services if they abused our son in any way. And we were successful. They were afraid of us and that helped to keep Charlie safe.

Your good relationship with your child and your ability to make sure the organizations that service your child know you will not accept any abuse of your child under any circumstances are truly the only weapons you have to protect your him or her.

Sixth, if you let pedophiles talk long enough, they will always implicate themselves. They want to admit what they've done; it's part of the compulsion. This was my experience when I investigated child abuse and neglect as a social worker.

Seventh, the current estimate is that upwards of 95 percent of all pedophiles have been sexually abused themselves. In fact, some of their modus operandi in abusing children comes directly from how they were abused.

For example, if Sandusky sexually abused children in a shower, it is likely he was abused in a shower.

If victims do not receive treatment, they may become predators themselves.

Eighth, the mental illness that makes pedophiles sexually abuse children does not go away without an intense intervention over years. Even then some never recover. It is a real psychological disorder. So to "watch them closely" or limit their access to children does not work. Only intense therapy helps.

Ninth, in some states in the United States and in some countries, there is a statute of limitations on the amount of time someone has to come forward after being victimized by a pedophile, that is, there is a restricted amount of time in which a person can report the abuse for the legal system to be able to do anything about it.

We all need to work to remove this limit so that when victims come back twenty years later, they have some legal recourse. I hope this has helped you to know better what some of the parameters of pedophilia are and what can be done.

WOMEN MOVING FORWARD®
CHAPTER 2
YOUNG WOMEN

A Need to Come Together to Talk and Celebrate
WMF® Graduates Newsletter January 2006

I participated in two luncheons recently that made it clear to me how much we need to come together as women.

The first was a fundraiser that featured Dr. Linda Silverman as guest speaker. Linda is a world-renowned expert on giftedness and gifted education. Her Gifted Development Center in Colorado is recognized as a resource for gifted information across the globe.

In her workshop Linda challenged the women attendees to explore how we felt about our giftedness and where we got those notions from. She also moved us closer to accept our giftedness.

As you know we use the "Gifted Woman as Imposter" article in every Women Moving Forward© workshop. This article reports that most gifted women feel like imposters; we think we aren't really gifted, but just good actresses. We have found in our work that most of us feel as if someday those with authority over us will find out the truth, and we will be exposed for the frauds we really are. Others of us would say we are "darn lucky" to have a career or job at all. That leads us to overcompensate by trying to be all things to all people. But I don't have to elaborate; you know it all to well. After all we live it every day.

It occurred to me when I was at the first luncheon one of the reasons intelligent, competent, gifted women need to be together with each other at luncheons or Women Moving Forwards© or The Women's Leadership Retreat© is that these are safe spaces for us to be as intelligent and as gifted as we are. We don't have to hide who we are, nor do we have to pretend to be less than we are.

The second luncheon I attended was to celebrate a friend's daughter's coming of age. She had turned thirteen and was developing into a beautiful, intelligent young woman. So we got together to celebrate her new life.

We gave her gifts for her new life; a pearl necklace and earrings and a copy of the latest version of *Our Bodies Ourselves* from the Boston Women's Health Book Collective.

We provided her with a safe space to be recognized for her intelligence and giftedness and we pledged to be there for her if she needed us.

Hopefully we also modeled for her what the first luncheon produced: a safe space for us to "come out," to be who we are fully and to celebrate what that means.

In this age of young women self-destructing through eating disorders, alcohol and drug addictions, and older women slinking off for massive amounts of plastic surgery to look younger, I think it is imperative for all of us to find safe spaces to "come out" and celebrate our intelligence and giftedness.

Getting Ready for The Real World /
My Message to Teenage Girls
WMF® Graduates Newsletter July 2007

The website www.smartgirlsrock.com asked me to write the article below for teenage girls. This is a wonderful website for young teenage women who want to feel good about themselves and their intelligence. I took the opportunity to tell them what I imagined you would want me to tell them about their future. You can access the article on their website as well as on our website.

For over twenty-eight years I have worked with very successful women in corporations worldwide like Proctor and Gamble, IBM, Johnson and Johnson, Hewlett Packard and Dell. They often say to me, "If I only knew at fifteen what I know now, I could have saved myself a lot of trouble".

Now I have the wonderful opportunity to tell you what these great women wish they had known at your age.

1. Expect to make mistakes at work and expect to be corrected for making them.

    Don't worry about making mistakes. Accept that you will make mistakes and be ready to hear bad things about yourself that a boss or co-worker will say. Practice apologizing and be ready for any and all correction. When people correct you they are doing you a wonderful service. They are telling you how they see you. This is invaluable feedback for you to have.

So be ready to not always be right.

2. Not everything will go your way all the time.

   Lower your expectations that your company will implement your suggestions or conditions. In fact, if you have 25 to 50 percent batting average, that is, your boss/company takes your suggestions and implements them 25 to 50 percent of the time, you are doing well.

   Learn to accept someone else's way of doing things now, because once you get out in the work world, you'd better be able to do your job the way others (your boss, company, and so on) have defined it. If you practice giving up some control now over how things will be done, it will be easier for you later.

   These days, most work is organized around projects that are run by multi disciplinary teams. Some of the women I work with are on two to three teams and must use influencing skills more than any other skill set. These skills include listening, confronting, clarifying and brain storming. If you learn these skills now you will be ahead of the game.

3. Temper your loyalty to your company with loyalty to yourself and your family.

   Work hard to establish yourself when you are in your first job, but don't forget your friends, family, and hobbies. In other words, have a life. Spend time with and on your friends, family and hobbies. Don't work all the time. Make sure you have downtime. Make sure you take care of yourself spiritually, emotionally and physically and make sure you are a multifaceted, whole person, not just defined by your job.

4. Finally, the women I work with recommend you prepare yourself for your first full time job.

   The best way I know for you to do this is to take a part-time job or internship while you are in high school. If you can do this only in the summer, that's fine; but do try out your wings now.

Most of all, I and the women I work with are excited for you because you have so much to look forward to. All of the growth you go through in the next few years will help prepare you for a wonderful, exciting future.

I warn you it goes quickly, so make sure you enjoy yourself and celebrate yourself as you go.

I wish you all the best for a successful and satisfying life.

WOMEN MOVING FORWARD®
CHAPTER 3
MOTHERHOOD

- Pregnancy Letter

- More from an Empty Nest

- Back in the Workforce or How to Prevent the Mommy Drain

- Is Motherhood Your First- or Second-Quarter Goal

- They Grow Up So Fast!

- L'Shanah Tovah: Happy New Year 5772 to All Our Fellow Jews

Pregnancy Letter
January 1989

Many years ago a friend of ours was pregnant with her first baby. I sent her this letter, hoping it would calm her down as she was scared about taking care of the baby after it arrived. Now many years later, hundreds of women have received this letter and have found it helpful when having their first baby.

You probably already know some of this stuff, but I wanted to send you a few helpful hints for after the baby's born - little things that were passed to me by others, or that I felt after Charlie was born:

1. Sleep when the baby sleeps – especially the first month or so. I think postpartum depression and anxiety are more likely if you don't get enough sleep. (More on that later.) When Charlie took a nap, it looked like a good time to work or clean, but it wasn't. Take a nap when the baby does.

2. Take maternity clothes to the hospital after delivery. You probably won't fit into your regular clothes at that point, so be patient with your body. Most women I know will tell you it takes a good year before they feel back to normal. Most doctors want you to believe six weeks. No way!

3. Be prepared to feel like you are totally unprepared to be left alone with your own baby. You may feel unskilled and untrained. Nothing you did in school or on the job will prepare you for this. None of those successes; dean's list, becoming a manager in a major corporation, will be

any help. Make sure you visit other women with babies regularly and talk it over with them.

4. My first outing with Charlie was on a hot day in June and I took him to K-mart. I wasn't used to carrying all the paraphernalia yet (another neat surprise – you will never leave the house again with just a purse). I managed to get me and Charlie into the K-mart okay, but when I came out and put everything in the car, keys, my purse, items I had bought and Charlie, somehow I pushed the locks down and locked Charlie in the car *with the keys inside*! Here was my precious "first baby" locked in the car on a hot day, so I summoned up all my training and communication skills and ran into the K-mart like a lunatic screaming hysterically that my son was locked in the car and I couldn't get him out and he was going to die.

   Well, we got him out, but I was so afraid I was not a good enough mother or careful enough mother that I told John he should not trust me with Charlie alone. I cried and cried. By the way, Charlie slept through the entire incident. When I told my story to my friend, Marion, who already had a two-year-old, she said, "I did the same thing. Go to the hardware store and get an extra key holder and put it under the front bumper of the car." It wasn't until Marion told me her story that I was willing to concede I was okay to handle my baby again. So the best offense for feelings of inadequacy is friends and family who have been through it all.

5. Along those same lines, if you turn out not to be an "earth mother" after the baby is born, or you don't like the pain of natural childbirth or nursing, you are not a bad mother.

You are just being you. Remember, too, that you can be who you are with your baby. I know women who desperately tried to breastfeed and had a terrible relationship with their baby because of it. Your relationship is the first priority; breastfeeding is second.

6. Last, but not least, I have yet to meet a mother who feels comfortable cutting her baby's nails for the first time (and those suckers grow fast). My mother used to cut mine when I was asleep. I gave the job to John. Remember, husbands, partners and grandparents are helpful. Let them have their own relationship with the baby. Go shopping at times, and let your husband, partner or the grandparents take over.

7. John and I don't know any better parent training manual than Parent Effectiveness Training by Dr. Thomas Gordon. We relied on it with Charlie and Adam, and we still do. It is the best Parent Education we know of. Read the book so you're prepared.

I hope some of this will be helpful later. You can always give me a call for a sanity check. Enjoy your baby. Life will be much more real and balanced now.

More From an Empty Nest

WMF® Graduates Newsletter November 2005

So far so good.

I get to visit my boys from time to time in their respective cities of Chicago and Los Angeles. I think I've captured some of the symptoms that, if not dealt with, can become full-fledged empty nest syndrome. Here are the issues I've discovered:

1. Have something to go to, or to go to more fully than you did before the Empty Nest. This has offset missing my daily "mom" role.

2. You must re-define your parenting role. You used to do it daily, now its sporadic, maybe weekly or monthly, and the nature of the relationship has changed. I am no longer all-encompassing Mom. I am now one of many experts they consult.

3. This is a process of leaving one role and going to another. My new role is slowly emerging for me, even with the increasing demands of the companies I run.

4. I require constant monitoring so I don't get drawn into the previous role.

    This is needed especially in two areas:

    a. Not becoming "Mom" again to my own sons, letting them fly away and take care of themselves. I've had to back off even where the boys' health is concerned. If

I took control back in any way, I'm back in the mom saddle again.

    b.   Not playing that mom role with other people around me. There are so many folks (including my husband) that are missing a mom, I can easily be drawn in. The urge to fill the empty nest is so strong, I believe it is primal.

5.   My new role is more of support and cheerleader as they take over more and more responsibility for their own lives.

As they climb their way to total independence, I get to stand on the sidelines and say "Great job!", "We're so proud of you and your abilities to _____" (fill in the blank here).

I am almost to the point where it is wonderful and a relief to not have them home. I'm not quite there yet, but I don't think it will take much longer!

Let me know your feelings and comments on this issue. I'd love to hear from you.

Back in the Workforce, Or,
How to Prevent the Mommy Drain
WMF® Graduates Newsletter January 2007

For many years, we have watched companies wake up to the fact that women who get pregnant are not automatically bad or incompetent employees.

Two recent articles in the Wall Street Journal (September 28, 2006) and Newsweek (September 25, 2006) point up the problems companies are still having in dealing with employees who are also mothers. The articles focus on the problem employers have with trying to lure new mothers back to work after their maternity leave. Apparently, women are using their new life changes to evaluate and augment their lives. What a concept; women actually taking time to think through their lives!

Employers, beware. This could become a trend. Women thinking and assessing you and your work environment could leave you coming up short. Or, maybe there's a way to have them want to return to you after the baby arrives.

For starters, make the transition easy, that is, the transition before the birth should be easy and the transfer back to work should be even easier. Have your human resources develop off-ramps and on-ramps that work and are kinder and gentler. Don't forget to train management. For example, if a woman tells you she's pregnant and going on maternity leave, it's probably not a good idea to say to her, "Oh darn, we're really busy now." So HR, take a role in this, please.

There are also companies with clearly written manuals for working mothers and fathers on maternity leave, policies, sick children, and so on. It's not a bad idea that every manager has one. Our

Women Moving Forward® graduates in a company in one country put one together that was also adopted in a different country by another group in the same company.

Good managers visit the Mom and baby many times while they are on leave to smooth the transition back. They also give first-time moms a chance to catch their breath and get over the feelings of guilt when they leave their baby for the first time.

There are other issues companies need to tackle as well.

- Don't offer a new mom a re-entry job in which she has to be away from her new baby for a month.
- Don't offer her a lesser job, unless she asks for it.

And, for Pete's sake, discuss all of this proactively with her before maternity leave begins.

You may also want to have her check with women you know at the company who have done it successfully, so she can get support from other working moms. That's why women's support groups, in your company are important.

In summary, companies who want to keep their women through their maternity leaves and after need to understand that women more than men, have non-linear work patterns. We don't start with a company and then continue to retirement.

But guess what, if companies can get use to the non-linear work patterns of women, they'll be ready to have Generation X and Y employees because they're as non-linear as they come.

Let us know what ideas you have to pass along to other women and how you feel about this.

Is Motherhood Your First or Second Quarter Goal

WMF® Graduates Newsletter January 2008

Tuesday, November 27, I read the Wall Street Journal as I do everyday. There is a section called "Home & Family," written by Sara Schaefer Munoz. She was reporting on a new "logical decision model" developed by a student and a professor at Duke's School of Business.

Sara reported that the model was designed to help women "determine the optimal time to conceive by balancing the benefits of motherhood against its effects on career and social interests and organizational concerns."

Some of you know I struggle daily with the real world applicability of some of the new ways women are approaching their lives. For example, the notion that anyone with family responsibility and a high-powered job can actually "balance" them is ridiculous and comical at best. I found this out as we raised two sons while I was building and running two successful businesses. So, I know that balance is not something to strive for, sanity maybe, not balance.

So, when this professor and her student decided to "help women" by developing a tool for them to measure exactly when they should have a baby, I can truly say; we have gone too far!

As a social worker I say that if you need a tool to decide when to have kids, you should not have kids until you are over your obsession with only having them when they will fit into your life. Kids don't fit in. If you parent well your children will be the focus of your life for as long as they are at home with you and then intermittently for the rest of your life. Parenting is a lifelong job.

It changes form from stage to stage, but it is always a part of who you are and should be!

In other words, if you cannot make a decision about having a child and when to have one without a management tool, how will you be able to make the thousands of decisions you need to make *daily* when you have a child? This type of decision isn't logical, nor should it be.

Hopefully women of childbearing age will forget about this newest attempt at applying organizational management strategies to their personal life and just go ahead and get pregnant when they want to. Your career will get handled no matter what. Trust me. I've been through this twice.

They Grow Up So Fast!
WMF® Graduates Newsletter March 2011

On June 13, 1981, I went to the hospital. My water had broken and it was my due date.

Our problem wasn't getting pregnant. It was staying pregnant. I had had a miscarriage at five and a half months with twins who were too small to survive. A specialist had told me I probably wouldn't be able to carry to term.

Finally I had found a great OB GYN, Paul Wexler, who diagnosed what had happened and said I should try again.

I made a characteristically Susan declaration that my next pregnancy would be successful, not just normal, but successful! My child would be born on their due date or later and would not be a preemie.

So, on that June 13 (my mother's birthday and my god daughter's birthday) Charles Tyler Van Vleet was born. He had an equally large Hebrew name but at nine pounds, thirteen ounces, he was big enough to carry those names.

This June 13 is Charlie's thirtieth birthday and we will be celebrating his very special day with him and his girlfriend, Megan.

When I see my oldest son I see a man who has become exactly what we had hoped: smart, loving, purposeful and a good human being.

I can recount all thirty years in my mind from birth to today, all the good and bad. And I know it's a cliché, but it goes so quickly!

So those of you with young children or those of you who have children you are close to in your work or your family, spend time with them now because when they turn thirty you will not feel like you spent too much time with them.

Happy thirtieth birthday, Charlie. As I said in your twenty-first birthday letter, you met *all* my expectations long ago and I hope now you are meeting your own expectations.

L'Shanah Tovah: Happy New Year
5772 to all our fellow Jews
WMF® Graduates Newsletter October 2011

As the New Year approaches (September 28-29), we Jews usually begin the process of evaluating the last year of our lives. This evaluation often includes a full accounting of our actions and how purposeful we were during the previous year.

And in preparation for the Day of Atonement, Yom Kippur, we look at what we have done that wasn't so good.

John and I typically review our lives and share with each other our individual evaluations and we evaluate our marriage as well.

We look at what we have accomplished and what we have not accomplished that we wanted to.

We also look at who we may need to ask for forgiveness because of anything we may have done to make someone's life more difficult. We do this with our sons as well these days, by conference call.

Sometimes I have to ask for forgiveness from them for not living up to who I think I should be as a mother.

If you are not doing this with your kids, partner, wife, or husband, I advocate you do. You can do it at some important time in your calendar.

Here's how we do it. We ask;

- What do you want to be acknowledged for?
- What do you want to acknowledge someone in the family for?

- What did you not accomplish that you wanted to complete?
- What do you want to be forgiven for?

All family members answer each question and then we move on to the next question. This exercise opens up the communications between you and your significant other and between you and your children.

It allows you all to take responsibility for what you have accomplished and what you have not accomplished and it allows you to see if you model the same. This in itself is a very powerful model for kids to see.

The most impressive answers typically don't come from me or from John, as witty as we can be. What the boys say to each other is most profound.

At least once a year, John and I become privy to how they feel about each other and the respect they hold for each other's way of life. It is awe inspiring.

In the beginning we heard Charlie tell Adam he wanted to be forgiven for fighting with him. And Adam told Charlie he wants to be forgiven for baiting Charlie.

Now it is mostly about how much they appreciate the other for their talents.

Again, incredible.

It also helps to be forgiven by your child for not living up to being the kind of mom you want to be.

First, this makes you say publicly what you didn't do or did wrong to the very people you think you slighted.

Second, it gives the children an opportunity to tell you how they feel about that. By the way, it usually goes like this: " But, Mom, I never wanted you to do that."

As a parent you get an opportunity to match up what you think you should be and do what they really want. *Priceless!* It's a true guilt reliever.

So, if you would like to try this, go ahead, and let me know how it goes. If you already have something like this in your family, let me know how yours works.

By the way, last year when we did this with a twenty-nine year old Charlie and a twenty-four year old Adam. Charlie said, "I hope to do this with my family someday."

No higher acknowledgment exists for parents.

WOMEN MOVING FORWARD®

CHAPTER 4

MEDICAL ISSUES AND HEALTHCARE

- Doctors, Doctors, Doctors
- A Physical Link to the Perils of Abuse

Doctors, Doctors, Doctors
WMF® Graduates Newsletter May 2008

For more than twenty years, I have been very faithful about getting my yearly mammogram. Both my grandmother and my mother had breast cancer. So from forty years old on I took myself to the mammography center at one of my local hospitals.

So once a year for more than twenty years I have had my breasts mashed into the vice that is mammography. The machine is essentially the same as it was twenty years ago, in terms of what I have to endure to complete the test.

Yes, there have been changes in x-rays to a digital format, so my films are now given to me on a disc. Wow! How wonderful? But I'm still being mashed and bruised to get the pictures now in a disc format.

Over the years, I have told anyone who would listen that if a man's penis had to be mashed like my breast to complete a medical test, no man would go, or the medical community would find some way to make the test less painful.

Okay, now I'm making a public plea to some of you engineers and scientists: please do something, anything, to figure out a way to make mammography less painful and at the same time more effective diagnostically.

If we can put a man on the moon, I figure we can find some way to do mammography without hurting every woman who takes the test.

Several years ago the mammography tech told me that, an engineer, was there when his wife had her mammogram. Apparently he was so upset by what he saw, he began to research another way to do the test.

So far I guess he hasn't been successful. I hope he is still trying!

In the meantime, I'll keep going for this rack-like torture and every time I will wonder what all of you with smaller breasts than mine must be enduring.

Let me know how you feel about this. And whatever you do, keep going for your test. It is the only diagnostic tool with any certainty that we have.

A Physical Link to the Perils of Abuse
WMF® Graduates Newsletter July 2012

I was reading the *Wall Street Journal* this past Tuesday and saw an article on Protein in the brain and it's effects on adaptability. Of course I'm now thinking of our Managing Corporate Change© workshop and research so I dove into this article.

To my surprise, there is a section on "cellular signs of abuse." Apparently the chronic stress levels women feel in abusive relationships can trigger DNA changes associated with aging.

In fact, the study they were quoting found that the length of abuse and whether a woman also had children who were also exposed to violence made the DNA changes associated with aging worse. The study concluded that "domestic violence affects women's health long after the abuse has ended."

Let me remind you, they are saying that being exposed to abuse causes DNA *damage*.

Now we have conclusive physical evidence for what those of us who work in this field knew was true psychologically: if you are abused or come from an abusive family you will carry that with you for the rest of your lives, and, it may prematurely age you.

As you can attest, I repeatedly warn young women who take Women Moving Forward® that they may not live to be my age if they keep up the life style they are living: trying to be perfect in everything without thought to how this is affecting themselves physically, or psychologically.

There was no part of the study that discussed self-abuse and it's effect on a woman, but I suspect the level and length of time you abuse yourself with this notion of being perfect will also count as abuse that changes your DNA, given what I have seen.

That coupled with abuse from someone else (and that is common with women who present clinically with a need to be perfect) is probably the kiss of death literally.

So essentially the study found that women, when subjected to abuse for any length of time with children or without may have DNA damage far beyond their years.

I conclude then that the sooner you leave the abusive situation the better. GET OUT! And, take your children with you.

The stress of starting over alone or as a single parent is not as detrimental to you as staying.

Moreover I wonder how you are faring if your company is also abusive. If you spend twenty years in an abusive company do you also get DNA damage that causes premature aging?

Isn't it like being in an abusive domestic relationship with regard to your physical wellbeing?

Well, I think we can say it probably is, given we have seen the same symptoms exhibited in women in this situation as we have in women coming from domestic violence situations.

I think this study has wide implications for all of us.

Bottom line: if you are a woman in an abusive situation, *get out!* It is life threatening if you don't.

WOMEN MOVING FORWARD®
CHAPTER 5
POLITICS

The Dixie Chicks and Other
Attempts to Shut Women Up

WMF® Graduates Newsletter March 2007

I can remember when the beef industry tried to sue Oprah for her comments about not eating hamburgers anymore. It was clearly an attempt to silence a woman with power.

Now we have an attempt to silence the Dixie Chicks. This is less a political statement and more about attacking women brutally to shut them up.

Yes I know the "Chicks" said something horrible about the president of the United States, but so do Letterman, Leno and Stewart, male comedians who berate our president nightly on TV shows that reach a world-wide audience of millions. It seems no one is calling for us not to watch their shows. But for a group of three women, they not only call for a CD boycott, they also systematically cut the group off from airtime on all country-western radio stations in the United States. And, when they got done with this idiocy, the Dixie Chicks had a number-one album and three new Grammies.

I'm sixty now, so I can recall many attempts to silence me as well. Some very important people in some very powerful companies and organizations have tried to put me out of business or cut me off from the women and men in their companies. But they have had to face the truth: this only makes me more attractive to their employees, because people do know the truth when it's spoken.

We welcome people communicating their points of view to us, we even reprint some in our newsletters. But never have we tried to silence someone for saying something about us. This is mainly because we believe in the ability of people both to hear the truth in whatever is being said and to recognize a lie.

So to those who might want to shut us up, beware. Women don't shut up so easily. You might say we have a way of using what you do to us to forward our work and to keep on going, no matter what you do to us. We are more resilient than you know.

See, women go through all kinds of things in their lives that are infinitely worse than anything you can do to us. Try childbirth, for example.

Let us know what you did about being attacked and how you used it to forward your work.

The World Is Watching Us
WMF® Graduates Newsletter March 2008

Many of you have asked how I feel about our upcoming presidential election. Questions have come not only from U.S. citizens asking how I feel about what is happening. Those of you in Europe, Asia, Central and South America have also asked me what I think about having Hilary Clinton and Barack Obama in the race.

Your very questions make it clear that we are no longer isolated, any of us, in our own little countries and our own little political status in our countries. We are all open to worldwide interest, because we are in a global world.

We in the United States have been so far behind some of other countries in our acceptance of women and people of color in our leadership positions in federal government. For example, Israel, India, Great Britain, and, Chile are only some of the governments that have been led by women.

In this regard, it is as if the United States has been a stubborn younger child refusing to be part of the modern world.

But finally we are catching up, and we have a very real chance of having a woman or an African-American man as the president (of course, that is if John McCain doesn't win).

When you ask me how I feel about this, it is hard for me to answer without it bringing tears to my eyes. I'm sixty-one, and I truly thought that this would never happen in my lifetime. I never thought I would see even the possibility of a woman or a person of color leading my country.

So I can answer you now: I feel grateful.

Grateful that my future grandchildren will live in a country in which anyone can run for president. That phrase is not just rhetoric anymore. It is now very real.

I am truly grateful that I may live to see a major change in the way the United States sees itself. Thank you to all of you who asked, and thanks for your concerns and interest.

I Apologize

I guess I should confess to all of you worldwide that I am as guilty as Judge Sotomayer, the nominee to our U.S. Supreme Court. If she is accepted, she will be only the third woman in US history to have this honor and the first Latina.

I have often said that women do some things better than men. I not only say it loudly and clearly, I saw it often. By the way, the research on the differences between male and female brains supports this idea.

Not only that but, I have also belonged to many women's groups including NOW and I hold life memberships in two others: National Council of Jewish Women and The Women's Cancer League.

Moreover, I run two female programs and have run one of them for more than thirty years. Men are not prevented from coming but we do discourage it, because only one man in the thirty-year history of Women Moving Forward made it through the course. And that's because he was a sponsor in Alcoholics Anonymous for women, so he already knew the level of emotional response women had. Three other men left on day 2 because they couldn't handle the raw emotion coming form the women participants in the room. They couldn't handle that you were all expressing it at the same time as a group.

Let the stoning begin. Susan Van Vleet discriminates against white males!

Just talk to the three I have lived with (including two I gave birth to) and I bet they can tell you lots of stories of how I discriminated against them. John, Charlie and Adam when called to testify against me make sure you tell them all about your bitch of a mother/wife, who hates you so much because you were white and male.

Those of you not from the United States and not schooled in our brand of sarcasm that's just what this is sarcasm on my part. I've been reduced to the use of sarcasm because I am so frustrated and upset with the conversations around Judge Sotomayer.

I cannot believe we are still having this stupid conversation in 2009. And by the way, when did white males as an affinity group become "at risk"? Someone has to fill me in on that one!

Are other countries so ahead of us in the gender game that they do not see the judge's statements in a speech or her membership in a woman's group as something that would disqualify her as a US Supreme Court judge?

Many countries in the world already have had women chancellors, prime ministers and presidents including many in Latin America.

What makes us so fundamentally backward and stilted in this arena? I am asking the question because I don't have the answer.

Please let me know how you feel. This latest craziness about Judge Sotomayer's membership has me stopped in my tracks. *Help!*

Feedback: "I Apologize"
WMF® Graduates Newsletter August 2009

We received some interesting comments back from the July WMF® newsletter. The following feedback is from the United States, Turkey and India.

I think you will enjoy the diverse points of view.

> Susan,
>
> Even though I no longer have an organization, every time I receive and email from you, I feel good. It reminds me of how much good you do in the world and how happy I am that I was the beneficiary of it. It always creates a moment of self-evaluation - so healthy for my soul!
>
> WMF® graduate

> Susan,
>
> I am with you on Judge Sotomayer. While I feel concerned with judges that legislate from the bench in general, I have listened to her rationale around some of her cases that have been overturned. She is not the racist that they have portrayed in the conservative media. That is so crazy making IMHO.
>
> She has ruled on some legal grounds that most conservatives would agree with. I find that

amazing. The nuances of law are complex, and there have been many games around this review.

What I find truly amazing is that if it were not political, and the name was left off her resume, she is the most qualified judge in this country! She would be hired in a heartbeat.

WMF® graduate

Hello Susan,

Thank you so much for all that you are doing for me. I read the newsletter.

I appreciate your views regarding Sotomayor. In India we have had a woman prime minister, Indira Gandhi. Our president now is Mrs. Pratibha Patil (first for India). [They are], women in prestigious positions, yet the status of women is still mediaeval.

Low literacy rates, very few property and inheritance rights, domestic violence and discrimination in wage rates are some of the many problems women face in India.

Sonia Gandhi, president of UPA, the ruling party, has to hear so many adverse comments from opposition because she is a woman and more so because she is an Italian. She is the widow of Rajiv

Gandhi and daughter-in-law of Indira Gandhi and a woman of steel.

We need women like her and like you. Together we all can try our best to minimize injustice and discrimination.

My mom-in-law used to say, "It's wrong to do injustice, but it is worse to bear injustice."

With warm regards and gratitude

WMF® graduate
India

Susan,

Your (sarcastic) questions are too tempting to not give at least a short answer. I have many other things I have to do, and I won't be a woman moving forward if I don't get going and do them!

You know all this stuff already, but you just got a little hooked, I think, when you got rudely jarred into noticing once more how unenlightened and closed-minded many in high places are, how much they don't know what they don't know, and how *maddening* it is.

Years ago in some anthropology studies I was reading, I learned that in many primitive tribes there were special ceremonies attended only by the men. The taboo against having a female anywhere near or giving a woman any hint as to what was going on was very, very serious and probably life threatening. They would bring out some musical horn-like instruments and blow loud scary sounds through them. They had some purpose in worshiping or placating gods, perhaps, but the anthropologists decided that their most important use was to scare the women!!! Scare them and make them think that the men had some special powers that they, the men, knew they were faking.

Why? The writers explained that the men were deep-down terrified of the power of the women. It was acknowledged that they had stronger muscles and bodies, but the women had the very mysterious power to bleed spontaneously with no injury to explain the bleeding. On top of that, they were able to produce new human beings. I suspect they also got the idea very clearly that women could intuit things and appear to mind read what a man was thinking and how he would react in any circumstance.

And just think of the power of women to draw them in sexually. I have always suspected that men believe, unconsciously at least, that women are aware of and use their sexual allure on purpose, much of which may well be based on pheromones that the woman doesn't even know she produces. She innocently walks past him, and he's suddenly attracted, even though he had no such intention.

Women experience the same thing, of course, but they are not so [susceptible to] the effect of it. Women also are not so likely to feel challenged by a man's allure. It doesn't make them feel inferior and controlled, but men do, and it worries them and makes them mad. I doubt they were, or are, able to consciously admit to any of what they fear are female superiorities. Nevertheless feminine powers were creepy, unexplainable and very scary. I think that is why they used their superior bodily strength to suppress the women and even went to the lengths of inventing secret sounds from the gods, and whatever. The only problem with this is that in certain historical times, including ours, women have let them get away with it for various reasons of their own, and then some women got so much of it, or their men became abusive enough to really put them down, that I'm afraid some women, themselves, came to believe in the superiority of men. That is a tragedy, especially as those women have led their male and female children to believe this myth too. The method of bringing religion into it in many cases was another trap.

Many of us are women successful in many ways, but if you think about it, almost all of us were up against some degree of discrimination at some time or other. And we came up with various ways to overcome. We could organize, go to conscious-ness raising groups, read, write, preach, march, holler, yell and invent women's studies depart-ments, diversity training, and so on. We could also ignore it and just get on with it, finding ways over, under, around the barriers, lots of things. Many of our methods have been very successful, but your upset over the ridiculous questioning of our honored candidate just goes to show us that it's still the same to some degree in some places.

As you know, I'm living in Turkey. When I came to medical school here because as a woman I couldn't get in in the States back in the 50's, it seemed perfectly natural for them here to admit women, and my class was filled with them, as were classes in pharmacy, law, engineering, whatever. In spite of that, we're now in a time of all sorts of abuses of women and plenty of controversy about it.

Those are some of the thoughts I have had about the question of why or how we got that way. But I don't even have a clue about the deeper why of how we could have become the way we are. And I agree with your outrage and sarcasm.

My mom tells me about an incident when I was just a toddler in which I got furious at the boy next door. He had been born just twenty-four hours before I was, so we were the same age. I was singing a song popular at the time, called "Flat Foot Floogie (with a Floy Floy)." He tried to sing along, but all he could do was run around the yard saying, "foy doy, foy doy." I stamped my foot and yelled, "He's so stupid he can't even say, 'Flat Foot Floogie!'" Guess what? That's pretty much the way it's continued to be with many of the men in my life and in my government. However, there are wonderful men and women everywhere of many colors who can say, "Flat Foot Floogie" far better than I can. And I've learned more effective responses than stomping my foot and yelling. But sometimes I still do.

Love,
WMF® graduate
Turkey

Blood Libel
WMF® Graduates Newsletter February 2011

For most of the last 3 years, since Sarah Palin was named the vice presidential candidate for the US Republican Party, I have stayed silent about her incredible rise to political power.

In the United States she has become a voice for the Tea Party and the conservative movement. I felt it was not okay to weigh in on her even when folks asked me about it because I don't believe in women fighting each other politically.

But now she has purposely used terminology that I hoped I would never again hear in my lifetime and she used it to refer to herself.

For those of you who are too young to remember, the ugly anti-Semitic claims against Jews, let me explain what it refers to. Blood libel or blood accusation was a false claim that Jews were killing Christian children to use their blood in Jewish ceremonies like the baking of matzo for Passover.

When a Christian child died, all Jews who had come in contact with that child were held responsible for his or her death. It gave anti-Semites the permission to kill Jews or to discriminate against them.

Just so you don't think this has never been used in my lifetime, let me tell you I was attacked almost every day from fourth grade on with this accusation and worse. I was called a Christ killer, a dirty Jew and a Christian child killer.

Some of my fellow classmates asked to see my horns and tail, another way of saying Jews are the devil incarnate. To Jews, blood libel terminology is as bad as the "N" word is for African Americans.

I cannot believe Sarah Palin had the chutzpah to use this term to refer to what a sheriff in Arizona said about her and her website language. (By the way she took it down.)

Either she is too stupid to realize what she was saying or she knew and she used it anyway. Either way she is an inappropriate as a United States presidential candidate. There are too many other Republican candidates worthy of our attention.

Two Women to Admire
WMF® Graduates Newsletter March 2011

Tonight as I sat at my computer I got one of those alerts from a news agency. It said Geraldine Ferraro had died at seventy-five.

For those of you too young to remember Geraldine, long before Sarah Palin, she was the first woman to be nominated by a major party to run for vice president of the United States.

I remember vividly the media response to her nomination. Friends of mine who worked for newspapers at the time swore to me she did not have the resume to do the job credibly. Does this sound familiar?

She ran and with great humor and patience she answered stupid question after stupid question. I thought she won her debate as well but apparently no woman at the time could win any debate as far as the pundits were concerned.

I saw her speak later in her life about her experience and what she had learned. It was stunning that she took in stride her position as role model to women at that time and continued to model a full life with husband, children and political role.

Another US woman in politics who was also a wonderful role model for all of us was Shirley Chisholm. Shirley was the first African American woman elected to Congress and the first woman candidate for president from the Democratic Party. Yes, America she was *before* Hilary Clinton.

I was lucky enough to hear her speak as well. She spoke eloquently about what it was like to run as a woman and an African

American. She knew great discrimination from her own party as well as the opposition. She had to fight to be included in the debates and she was a stellar debater.

Women from many other countries already have or have had a woman heading up their government. But we, in the United States, we have yet to experience this.

So when I read about Geraldine's death today I wanted to pay tribute to her and to Shirley for helping us get closer to having a woman in our top office. As candidates, they incurred the wrath of many and were attacked brutally by members of their own party but they persevered. And though they did not win they broke open the possibilities in all of our minds.

WOMEN MOVING FORWARD®
CHAPTER 6
MILESTONES

- In Memoriam

- Thirty Years

- Leisha's Moving Forward Experience

- A Message to Young Women

- A Year of Firsts

In Memoriam

Many years ago I met a woman at a convention. She was part of the Native American Rights Movement of the 1960's and as part of that, she was fighting for Native women's rights.

We talked for a while and I learned she was Cherokee. I told her about being a Jewish minority and she said she admired how we had our own systems in place for social services and education. I described how I went to Hebrew school three times a week to learn my history and the language of our religion. She marveled that we could get young Jewish kids to do that and she wanted very much to do something similar in the Native community.

Flash forward to today, with Native American colleges and programs on reservations to teach the language of the people as well as the history and customs.

Wilma Mankiller was a part of the development of all of that and more. She led a drive to institute health care and social services on tribal lands and negotiated a self-government agreement with the United States government. She was the first woman to lead the Cherokee Nation under the title of chief and one of few women in Native communities to hold that office.

She re-established the Cherokee custom of a matrilineal culture and used that to legitimize her leadership as part of the traditional Cherokee culture. She was a role model for young Native women all over the world.

I am proud to say she was a social worker like me and a community organizer par excellence.

She used to give speeches and would often refer to her last name, Mankiller. By way of explanation she would say, "It's my nickname and I earned it!".

She will be missed.

Thirty Years
WMF® Graduates Newsletter September 2008

The thirtieth anniversary of Women Moving Forward® is coming up in January 2009. It happens to coincide with our wedding anniversary, which is also thirty years.

When I was a young woman (and there is some debate about whether I was ever really young) I don't think I ever thought anything I did, except maybe having kids, would last for thirty years or more.

The workshop that I designed over thirty years ago and piloted in January, 1979 with thirty-eight women and two co-trainers was only supposed to last until women made it to all levels of organizations. It was not supposed to become a popular, if not underground, phenomenon thirty years later. It certainly wasn't supposed to be as applicable then as it is now.

Currently women from all over the globe are taking the course and applying its principles to their lives. I always knew we as women were really meant to be international in scope. We somehow know at our core that, no matter what country we are in, a woman is a woman is a woman.

We know that women all over the world have trouble focusing on themselves and we know that we are our own worst enemies sometimes. It is universally accepted that we, as women, must continue to press on no matter what has happened to us. So we give ourselves no time to integrate our successes and our failures.

Those of us with children and family responsibilities (which in almost all cultures I have studied goes first to the oldest female in the family) as well as business responsibilities also know that no woman ever balances her life. She just tries to survive with a modicum of sanity each day.

So why this would be such a success thirty years later should not be such a shock. But like all women this milestone will be hard for me to digest.

It is much easier for me to accept that I have been married to John for thirty years! That is, it is easier to account for all the hard work that it took to have a workshop last thirty years and still be making a difference internationally.

I would much prefer to say "I was just lucky" or "G-d blessed me" than admit that thirty years ago I looked into my soul and heart and mind and developed something that would contribute to women all over the globe for thirty years.

So, for me to integrate this accomplishment and to open this workshop up to as many women as possible in 2009, we will be doing the workshop and having celebrations for graduates of the workshop in many different locations in 2009.

Leisha's Moving Forward Experience
WMF® Graduates Newsletter October 2008

As many of you know, Leisha, my assistant, had the special honor of speaking to Michelle Obama, Joe Biden and other political dignitaries at an event during the Democratic National Convention in Denver.

So many of you asked me how Leisha's experience went with Michelle Obama. I asked her to write an article for this month's newsletter about her experience. As you will see from her article, it had a profound impact on her.

This is not a political statement or a support article for Obama and against McCain. No matter whom you support, this is an article about one woman's "moving forward" in her own experience of herself, something you all can relate to. Here's Leisha's experience:

> My moving forward was shown to me. It was reflected back to me by my participating in a Women's Economic Issues Forum with Michelle Obama, Senator Joe Biden, four women governors and three other working women from across the United States. We sat on a stage before an audience of about three-hundred people and lots of media. I was asked to share my story simply - the story of raising my son as a single parent and the importance his education. I did everything I thought at that time was necessary to ensure my son had the best education possible. But what I also did was put my own education and, moreover, my personal goals on the back burner. My son graduated from the University of Colorado in 2002.

I am in the process of detaching from his life and creating a life of my own.

Being a part of this select group made me more receptive to my own accomplishments and abilities. For some reason this interaction contributed to my belief in my personal legitimacy. I have always felt isolated and different from others. By legitimacy, I mean an awareness of who I am and that I do have a place in this world.

Michelle Obama exudes centeredness, sincerity and self-assuredness. Her sincerity and comfort in her own skin and her accomplishments became a mirror to me. It was an "I want to be like Mike/Michelle" moment for me. I have never had this kind of emotional association with another woman, except, an envy of someone's physical appearance or life-style. It is amazing to me that I have such strong feelings about a woman I met only once and spoke to directly for only a couple of minutes.

The moving forward for me was in looking in that mirror and acknowledging my feelings about that day and my life to that point, all my feelings and not being afraid or ashamed to feel them and to also share them with others. When Joe Biden walked across the stage, to me after the forum, congratulated me and shared some personal thoughts it held true for me that I was not alone and I could persevere.

I don't have a law degree, or a high level profession, or a remarkable husband or the love and admiration of those near and far, *but I have survived.*

I became a single mother at age nineteen, lived in subsidized housing for five years and then bought my own home. I have worked two and sometimes three jobs for over twenty-five years. I sent my son to the best schools in Denver. I ended an abusive relationship. I started my own company. I am surviving my only son's life transitions and I am currently attending college.

The meeting of Michelle Obama, a woman close to my own age but with what appears to be opposite life experiences, has made me believe that *I am enough.*

A Message to Young Women
WMF® Graduates Newsletter September 2011

We had my cousin's daughter and son-in-law staying with us last week. It was an opportunity to get to know them better and for them to get to know us. My cousin also visited from the other side of my family with her husband and son.

It was the vortex of family and it was fun and instructive *and tiring*.

I was asking the universe what I needed to learn from all the family contact last week. I was so tired the answer wasn't readily available.

Finally, last night it came to me. You see, I had done the unthinkable for any woman in my family. I had moved away and forged my own life.

That realization seemed so simple at the time, but as I look back on it, I can say it helped me find my own path in life and create my family the way I wanted to, without the pressure family and culture placed on the shoulders of the women who stay close.

Of course you can never quite be free.

Even little actions you do can come directly from your family and culture. For example, we took my cousin's daughter and her husband to lunch in Denver and both of us women ordered the same sandwich. As soon as they were put in front of us, Amy and I took the excess bread out of the top of the roll. Just that similarity in a small action comes from our family culture. We had never seen each other do that before, so it had an impact on both of us.

My cousin from the other side of the family sat down next to me at the cookout we did for the family to meet. She told me about her life and what was happening. We haven't seen each other for years so it was good to catch up but also interesting that she seemed to want my approval for how she had chosen to live.

When everyone was gone I told John, and he said that they want my life not my approval. He felt they wanted to be able to do what I had done: build the life I wanted to live, even if it was outside of the values of the culture we were all a part of.

Last night I realized that what I had done was not easy it was hard. I had purposely taken from my culture the rituals and values I wanted to have and left behind the ones that never worked for me. Sometimes that meant I was not valued in my culture and sometimes that meant I was.

In other words, I had become my own woman, still rooted in the culture I came from while following the new path I had chosen.

The ramifications of living this kind of life are great. You may lose contact with some family because of the path you choose. Yet, the rewards are greater. Being your own woman is it's own reward.

This life I live, while not completely free, works for me because I built it to do so.

I invite you to do the same. If you are a mother, I invite you to let your daughters do the same.

A Year of Firsts
WMF® Graduates Newsletter 2011

For some reason 2011-2012 seems to be a year of firsts for us and for our company.

1. We will be in Frankfurt Nov. 1-3 for both Women Moving Forward® AND Men, Relationships and Work© and no individual company is sponsoring them.

2. We will be in Singapore April 10-12 for the first time for Women Moving Forward®

3. I will turn 65 and move from my current health plan to a US Government Plan called Medicare.

4. We have 3 new clients who are totally new to our work and our workshops.

5. And, hopefully by January 1 there will be additional good news for our family.

So, what am I to make from all of these firsts?

I guess all of us need to be ready for big changes in 2012 and we need to embrace the spirit of them not reject them out of hand because they are new.

My sons, Adam and Charlie, pointed out to us recently how non-resistant we are to all the new technology that comes out daily. They said we are different from other folks our age because we tend to see the *possibilities* in the new technology and we find a way to use and integrate it into our lives and our business.

I think this has been my life-long belief that I should see the world and everything in it as a possibility of learning something new that can contribute to my life.

So many US citizens these days see people in other parts of the world as scary and as our competition because of the scarcity of all things.

They are afraid of all things not like themselves. In my profession, this is called xenophobia: the fear of strangers.

I think I am too old to start being xenophobic: I just don't have the energy to start now.

If you are afraid of going somewhere new, meeting new people, using new technology, and so on, stop and think for a minute and see if your fear is not based in reality.

WOMEN MOVING FORWARD®
CHAPTER 7
MARRIAGE

- A New Reality

- Response To: A New Reality

A New Reality
WMF® Graduates Newsletter February 2009

On February 10ᵗʰ John and I will celebrate our thirtieth wedding anniversary.

Recently some friends asked us how we feel about such a milestone. Frankly, I have no answer for that question.

For me, being married for thirty years is like an out-of-body experience. I can't believe it's been thirty years! I never thought I had it in me to be married this long! I often say to close friends that I would never do this again. That it has been one of the hardest things I have ever done. That if anything ever happened to John, that would be it for me. I wouldn't have another one of these.

By the way, this is a compliment to John: he was the only person I could see myself working this hard with.

It honestly feels like yesterday that we were married on Lookout Mountain in Golden, Colorado. We hadn't known each other for that long, only six months, but we were sure in only that amount of time.

I guess we were right. It has lasted for thirty years. Friends and family were not sure at all. To some of his friends I was, and I quote: "Yoko Ono taking John Lennon away from the Beatles". When my father found out John played rugby he warned me that those are "the crazy athletes who wear no pads and helmets while playing a football game."

They were not all good times. We can't say, like Dr. Phil McGraw and his wife Robin, that we've never fought or had bad times. We can say we both made big mistakes in the thirty years. But we did have something that helped our marriage last through bad times. Even the loss of twins during delivery, the formation of two businesses and the break-up of one of those businesses during the first year of our marriage didn't break us up!

We think it is because we had a purpose for our marriage that was bigger than us that kept us together, even when we couldn't stand each other.

When we married, we decided to contribute to others out of our marriage. We also had personal purposes that seemed parallel to each other and not at odds, so we decided to take the big leap after only six months of dating.,

During the hard times, we knew it wasn't just about us but about how we could contribute to others out of all that was happening to us.

We used the marriage to educate other women and couples about fertility and pregnancy, which no one was talking about thirty years ago.

Out of the differences in our cultures we used our coping styles with each other, including our listening skills, to help other couples deal with theirs.

Out of our problems with our son's learning disabilities and educators' lack of knowledge of same, we were able to help other parents to get the information they needed to get a proper education for their children.

And out of our arguments and disagreements came a whole lot of information for other couples to use.

Life is always full of surprises and twists and turns so get ready for it. You have heard me say in WMF® that there really is no such thing as balance. Balance is not something you can have in a long-term relationship either.

You just have to work it through day after day and keep the purpose of your marriage or partnership alive every day so you can focus on it and not on the billion a day reasons he or she irks you to death.

If you know what we are talking about, let us know how you have held it together and what has worked for you.

For those of you just starting out together, trust me when I say that it can be worth it if you put the commitment and work into it.

Response To: A New Reality, February Newsletter Article
WMF® Graduates Newsletter March 2009

Hi Susan,

I enjoyed your article on being married for thirty years. Congratulations! Jay and I have been married for eleven years (so not nearly the milestone you have achieved), but very happily married. What I mean is that we still miss seeing each other when he is at work for forty-eight hours or we are away from each other for several days. Of course we have our moments of wanting to ring the other's necks, but we work those out and move on.

For us, the key has been that we support one another in what the other person wants or needs to do for themselves. We are constantly growing and changing and we support each other in that change, meaning we make the sacrifices. For example, I supported Jay financially to get his master's degree. He went on to work in that field only to discover he loved the concepts, but the actual work in that industry was boring and he hated it. So we made some financial changes that allowed him to quit and stay home with Sarah until he figured out what he wanted to do.

After two years, he decided he wanted to be a career firefighter and that's what he is doing now. During the fire academy, I was basically a single parent. I didn't bitch at him about how hard it was; he knew what he was asking me do and in turn has given me space to do what I need for me: WMF, the leadership retreat, visiting my sisters, and so on.

So I guess the bottom line for us is that we support each other with what we need to do for ourselves. So we can take care of ourselves, enjoy our time together and enjoy our family time all because we both feel we can be ourselves and do what we need for our selves without being given a guilt trip.

WOMEN MOVING FORWARD®
CHAPTER 8
POINTS OF VIEW

- Differing Points of View
- My Recent Rants on Facebook

Differing Points of View
Memo to WMF® Graduates July 28, 2004

I know that some of you are angered and frustrated about our last few memos. Some of our graduates have very conservative views and beliefs and are committed to those. Some have asked us to remove them from our mailing list and they have every right to do so.

I must admit that there is a whole group of social issues for which, as I strive to be a good person and Jew, I do have "liberal" leanings.

Basic Human Rights, I believe, should be denied to no one, regardless of race, religion, ethnicity or sexual preference.

My family and my people did not die in concentration camps so that I could pick and choose what groups of people I believe have a right to live fully, even if I or you feel uncomfortable with them or their lifestyles.

I thought you should know I also believe this:

- People who abuse and neglect their children are bad parents.
- Managers who abuse people they manage are bad managers.
- People can change and often do.

And finally,

- People are basically good and when given real and clear options they will choose to better themselves and their families.

I believe all of this not because of my religious or political ideology, but because of my forty years of working with people from every walk of life.

People are people are people.

We all ultimately march to the same drummer and have the same issues to resolve. You may have had that very experience in Women Moving Forward®, the experience of a woman sitting across from you, from a completely different background, who was struggling with the same issues you were.

So I will respect you if you ask to be removed from our mailing list because of ideological differences. I believe you have every right to do that and I congratulate you on being committed to your values and beliefs, no matter how much mine differ from yours.

My Recent Rants on Facebook
WMF® Graduates Newsletter May 2011

If you have been following my most recent rants on Facebook you will have a clue that there are two things I hate and won't tolerate at my advanced age;

1. Lying, and

2. Negotiating in bad faith (such as telling a contractor you want one thing when you really want another).

My cousin Scotty says it's because I'm a "Jersey girl" and we're from the same family. I'm not sure that's it but okay I'll accept that as an explanation.

My reaction when you lie to me or negotiate in bad faith by lying is to blow you and the relationship up, causing me to decide that you cannot be trusted, that I can never do business with you again and certainly I cannot have you in my life or around my family.

Some of you have already had this experience with me and you can attest that, it isn't pretty. Long ago I determined I should not learn martial arts or own a gun, because I would not want to arm this mouth.

So some of you will not be surprised to hear that this is one of the biggest problems with many companies. Not only do employees lie, but company systems are also set up to lie (that is, SAP).

Years ago I tried to negotiate a contract with a company that shall remain nameless. Step one for me *before* negotiations was to do a legal search on the company with special attention to its lawsuits with suppliers.

I found out that the company negotiated for large volumes so they could get a deep discount per unit and then they made sure in the contract they had no penalty for ending the contract for any reason. They also made sure the supplier would have to sue them in the state they were in, which – for want of a better phrase – they owed.

Most of their law suits with suppliers were for this very issue. They would order ten million widgets at a deep discount because of the volume and then they would end the contract at five thousand widgets.

If you are in purchasing are saying "Yeah, so?" you have been so co-opted by your corporations lack of morality that you think this is just the way it is done. No, it's not. It is not "just the way it is done" to give a supplier a contract to sign that;

a. Is unsignable given the wording and the $3,000 cost to a small business like mine to have a lawyer change it is prohibitive; and,

b. says whatever we do for you, you own.

Your contracting and purchasing department seems to have the hope that we will be so awestruck by the thought of doing business with you that we will give up all our rights to do so.

As we used to say in Jersey "Not so fast, slick!" Some of us know better and I warn you I will not negotiate if you present me with nonsense like that.

I truly thought when I was thirty I would mellow out in my sixties, but the closer I get to "retirement" the more I refuse to entertain the lack of morality and ethics in the corporations we work with. I warn you: I get really cranky!

The crazy thing is how many of you contacted me thinking I was talking about your company. Many of you have shared with us how upset you are with your own departments and systems. You have shared your own frustration at trying to get suppliers paid in a timely manner.

Just to be crystal clear with you, I'm talking about *all* the corporations we deal with, yours and all the rest.

The excuses folks make when negotiating in bad faith are getting old and very comical. Here are some recent ones:

1. The royal wedding caused a delay.

2. We have an SAP system.

3. I have children.

4. Everyone is on vacation.

5. The address we gave you for the contract was wrong and now it will have to be re-done but you'll have to make your payable day start from today.

6. Our accounts payable is in (insert any country).

7. The country where you will do the training has very low salaries. I liken this to my mom trying to get me to eat

my dinner by telling me the children in (insert a country) are starving.

So, the next time you speak to me and you know you've done this, or your company has, I'd like an apology first. Then I'll be happy to speak with you.

All I'm asking for is the truth. The truth will do nicely, and I promise then I won't get cranky. Rather than hearing numbers 1-7 above, I'd prefer to hear, "We won't work with you or your company because of your attitude."

WOMEN MOVING FORWARD®
CHAPTER 9
WORKPLACE ISSUES

- Push Factors / Pull Factors

- Feedback on: "Push Factors/Pull Factors"

- Surprise! Surprise! Surprise!

- What the Heck Is Going On?

- Employer Retaliation and Other Stupid Mistakes

- Feedback on: "Employer Retaliation and Other Stupid Mistakes"

- Gossip

- Feedback on: "Gossip"

- Is Your Company a Tease?

- Feedback on: "Is Your Company a Tease?"

- Age Bias and Gender Bias

- Could Watson, the IBM Super Computer, Lead WMF®?

- Male Chauvinist Pigs, or *Les Phallocrate*

- Guess What? Women Are Valuable on a Team

Push Factors / Pull Factors
WMF® Graduates Newsletter September 2006

I know I have already told you about a great article from the March 2005 issue of the *Harvard Business Review* called: "Off-Ramps and On-Ramps; Keeping Talented Women on the Road to Success" by Hewlett and Luce.

It makes the point that women make choices regarding work and life all along their career paths and that companies need to know that and build careers around it if they want to meet the needs of women. I want to focus this month on their description of the factors: push and pull. They say in the article that these are the two categories women cite most as the reason to stay or leave their company.

- Push factors are the company issues women face that convinces them not to stay.

- Pull factors are personal and family issues that women face that convince them to leave their jobs.

For example,

Push Factors	Pull Factors
• under-utilization of a woman in her job • a bad boss • no praise or recognition for a job well done • negative or hostile work environment	• a sick child • a sick family member or elderly • family member • divorce • death in the family • family guilt

• increased responsibility with no commensurate title or raise or no acknowledgement of same	• internal guilt, such as in role as wife or parent
• sexual harassment towards the woman herself or women she knows	• guilt in role as church member or school or parental and grandparent guilt in parenting role
• constant demands and no acknowledgement	• child doing poorly in school
• forced moves and re-location with no support	• marriage • being the first person in the family to have a profession, not just a job

Given all the pull factors women face daily, companies always ask me what they can do to impact the attrition of women. They as, "Is it a losing battle?" And, "If family or cultural issues are the pull factors, as a company we don't have much control over that, do we?"

I tell companies that ask me these questions the following:

Given the enormous influence of the Pull Factors in every woman's life, you can impact the attrition of women at your company and control the impact on their personal lives by making sure their experience at your company is a very positive one.

No woman leaves a company she loves and that has proven to her she is valuable no matter what the pull factors are.

So for companies wanting to keep their attrition rates for women low or that want to attract excellent women candidates, here are some dos and don'ts:

1. Don't exacerbate or create push factors for women at your company, especially given all the pull factors they deal with daily.

2. Make sure women at your company are utilized fully. Underutilization is the number-one issue women give as a reason for leaving a company.

3. Get rid of dysfunctional bosses, wherever they are in your company and at every level. They become very big push factors and create attrition all the time.

   How do you find dysfunctional bosses at your company? Simply review attrition rates of managers regularly. If they are losing people regularly or they are losing all their women employees, they are dysfunctional and will keep your attrition numbers up.

4. When you promote a woman, promote her. Don't play around with the promotion. By that I mean, don't give her the increased responsibility without the commensurate title and pay. That is a push factor for women who deserve better.

5. Make sure you are attending to or have staff at your company that can attend to the needs of the whole woman. If she needs support with her family, listen and refer her for help. If she is having trouble with her child's health, listen and refer her for help. Just because you are her employer does not mean you are exempt from listening to her needs.

Sometimes a quick referral to someone can help make a female employee feel the company is not making her personal situation worse. The company is actually supporting her to get it fixed.

I will say it again: women don't leave companies and jobs they find satisfying: they leave companies and jobs they find unsatisfying.

Feedback on: "Push Factors / Pull Factors"
WMF® Graduates Newsletter October 2006

We want to thank those of you who sent us such wonderful comments on our "Push Factors / Pull Factors" article in the September WMF© Graduates Newsletter.

Many of you shared your personal experiences with us. You all had one thing in common: finally you had the words to express what has been going on for you and other women you know. And now that you have the words you can discuss it as a legitimate issue.

Here are the comments of one of our WMF® graduate's that I think summarizes so much of the feedback we got:

> Hello Susan,
>
> I just wanted to say "Thank you." For a long time I thought I was alone when it came to feeling the push/pull factors. In my last job I felt almost all of these factors.
>
> I felt under utilized, constant demand, a negative environment, no compensation for added responsibility, family guilt and internal guilt and was the first person in my family to have a career. I was forced to move to a new position and the balancing act did not feel good anymore.
>
> I did not love my new job enough to overcome the push/pull factors. It wasn't worth it anymore. I'm sad that it came to that point. I tried to explain this to people before, and they looked at me like

I was crazy. It's amazing how much better I feel not to be alone.

When Push/Pull Factors Converge: The Real Issue

To continue the discussion from last month's article, I wanted to be clear that it is never one issue or another that causes women to decide to leave; it is always a convergence of push and pull issues coming together that makes us throw up our hands and say, "No mas."

I think the feedback from graduates' points this out very clearly. In fact, it is a certain percentage of push factors plus a certain percentage of pull factors that causes this choice. For example,

Marion (a fictional woman working at a high-level management position in a Fortune 500 company) has a sick child and no good-quality child care (pull factor) and she has not received any feedback on the quality of her work from her boss for over nine months (push factor). The combination of these push/pull factors might make her decide to leave."

The convergence of the percentages from both the push and the pull factors is what tips the balance for women. It is not the sick child, no poor child care and the lack of managerial feedback; it is those particular issues converging on that particular woman. This is an important concept for management to understand. It's never one or the other issue or even the combination of same; it is the convergence of things on the woman that makes her throw up her hands.

It would be helpful for all women to know what their tipping point is. Look at what push factors and what pull factors converging would make you want to leave. It's always good to be prepared.

Surprise! Surprise! Surprise!
WMF® Graduates Newsletter August 2008

In the June 20, 2008 issue of *Entertainment Week* was an article by Mark Harris. The summary of the article is that the entertainment business is always surprised when a movie like *Sex and the City* does well. Harris chastises the business for being so stupid that they are surprised that yet another chick flick (a movie targeted at women) made so much money and was so successful.

I don't think the Entertainment Business is the only business group wide-eyed and shocked that women will come in droves for a product that is applicable and makes sense in their lives.

I'd say it is in good company with its sister businesses, the consumer products business, the pharmaceutical business, and the high-tech business (yes, women do buy tech products).

Many years ago, I had a conversation with a male vice president who told me women are fooled by the media into thinking they needed "wings" on their sanitary napkins. Women, he believed, were buying his competitor's product with wings because they were being influenced by advertising.

The point is that we need to start telling our companies not to be surprised anymore when women buy something they see will make their lives easier or more fun. Wings on sanitary napkins were a wonderful development that helped us keep the napkin in place so we weren't constantly experiencing leak.

Stop telling us what we want; give us what we really want and need. And while we're at it, stop trying to blame us (women) for the failure of your products. If you products are failing with women, it's probably because women don't like them or don't want to spend money on them.

Conversely, if your products are selling to women it isn't because the planets have aligned or because you had the best advertising on the planet. It is more likely that someone in product development knew what women wanted and designed the product for that. So consequently, we are buying it.

As Harris says about executives in the entertainment business, "When industry professionals are rendered wide-eyed with shock by the same piece of information again and again, only two explanations are possible: They're either....stupid or deeply invested in pretending that the power of the female movie going audience is.....surprising". I believe Harris has hit the nail on the head with this statement. They are deeply invested in pretending to be surprised that the female audience and the female consumer have power!

If the executives of any industry that sells to women can keep on pretending they are surprised then they never have to face the truth: in the market-place, women are powerful.

Many years ago we heard that a beer industry had done a study of who actually buys the beer, one of the products universally accepted as a "male" beverage. What this group found after exhaustive study was women bought 70 percent of all the beer consumed and 50 percent choose the beer at point of sale; they didn't just buy what their men folk told them to buy. That's right, women buy the beer and they decide which beer to buy.

What did the executives do with this new market place information? Did they revamp sales and marketing strategies? Did they assemble a female focus group to further look at this phenomenon? No, they simply dismissed the research they had paid for as ridiculous!

If executives actually faced the fact that women have marketplace power even in buying the beer, they would have to give up the fantasy that women are not as powerful as they are. We all know this would change their lives forever and their companies as well.

I think every executive selling to women should hear that one over and over. Stop being surprised. Just do your job and make effective products for 51 percent of the population.

What the Heck is Going On?
WMF® Graduates Newsletter June 2009

In over thirty years of doing business with over two hundred multi-national companies, we are seeing a return to a phenomenon we have not seen since the 1970's.

Women are being used to shore up men in higher positions. The way it works is women are asked to stay at the same level but to keep reporting to a new male boss that the company knows doesn't know the job as well as the woman they assign to him.

To a certain extent, the woman is actually babysitting her male boss.

Obviously the company feels she has the skills to do the job herself, or they wouldn't have put her in charge of her superior.

Then, after she does a wonderful job of training her boss and making sure he doesn't make a horrible mistake, she is rewarded with a bad performance review and may be given a demotion or even an invitation to leave the very company that put her in the position to begin with.

It appears to us that the men these women are assigned to get upset with the women knowing more than they do and so they try to punish them for being competent as they try to get rid of them. It's almost like they are trying to get rid of the evidence of their own incompetence.

We want to make it clear that we are not talking about one company here. It is happening across the corporate landscape and internationally as well.

It looks like an epidemic to us.

Part of the problem is when the woman is approached to take on this "opportunity," she is promised a promotion or a plum assignment when she finishes. Of course she's never promised anything in writing and expectations are never made clear.

If there is something I would recommend to deal with being put in this position it's don't take the role without a written contract. Make sure the company knows what you expect out of this assignment and make sure you have, in writing, some protection for yourself.

On second thought the best advice is, don't take the role at all. Tell them you can do the job yourself and ask them for the title and the raise.

If they won't promote you, then don't baby-sit the man they have promoted. Don't become a part of that crazy paradigm to begin with.

If you are already in one of these jobs, get out ASAP. Let the man you have been supporting do his own job and do what is best for you. Enough already! It should not be your job to make your superior capable of doing his job, not under those circumstances.

For HR folks, I suggest you take a close look at where this is happening in your company and do something, especially if a woman in this scenario is being threatened with her performance appraisal by the very man she has supported. I bet this could be bad for your company.

By the way, don't forget that the women in your company are watching and how you treat women will be noted by all of us. Trust me. This stuff gets around and women start refusing to fill positions in which they will be expected to fulfill this role. And this will have a severe effect on your company's ability to retain talented women.

Employer Retaliation and
Other Stupid Mistakes
WMF® Graduates Newsletter November 2009

According to the EEOC, in 2008, 23 percent more charges were filed against employers who allegedly retaliated against employees who filed discrimination complaints.

Not only is it illegal to retaliate against an employee who files a complaint, it's darn stupid. It makes everyone angry. And, trust me, everyone is watching. To those of us in the business, it also means the original complaint was probably true. If it weren't, why would the company need to retaliate?

But there are more important mistakes being made these days. Why are companies laying off or pushing employees out or demoting them while they tell the employees they are at fault for their own lay offs, pressures to leave, or demotions?

This is the stupidest thing any company could do. We even know that some managers in some companies are falsifying performance appraisals to do this. Now, I think we can risk saying that's illegal.

But worse than the legal ramifications (in case your employees decide to sue you) are the moral issue you will have with both the people who are victims and the people who are not.

The costs to a company for this kind of stupid activity can include the following:

1. Folks will leave the company angry or feeling incredibly incomplete with you, the company. Smart companies know that those who leave are still representatives of the

company. Just imagine if you squeeze out 1,500 people, and those 1,500 tell ten people how badly their company treated them in the end. The conservative estimate is that you then have 15,000 possible customers of your products or services angry with you. I know you can get the gist of where this is heading: reduced sales.

2. You are perpetrating a lie: that employee you are demoting, pushing out, or laying off did something wrong to force this action on the company's part. Not only is this immoral, it represents a bold-faced lie. See number one above for the effects of lying to employees who leave and multiply that by the number who are angry but stay.

3. The survivors are so guilty and scared, productivity goes down. How does that happen you ask? Let me describe it to you: The survivors are now worried they will be next. So let's say conservatively they spend ten more minutes a day in gossip, fear-based activity or just plain fear. Now multiply that by the number of survivors. Get the picture?

4. You are now asking fewer people to do more work. The amount on everyone's plate goes up exponentially. We already see an increase in stress-related conditions, like sleep deprivation. For example, when people don't get a good night's sleep, the first thing that goes is problem solving; the second is creativity. Good luck running a company these days where the problem-solving abilities of at least 25 percent of your employees are reduced and creative abilities are disappearing. There are *big costs* to what you are doing and no SAP solution will fix this one.

It's frustrating for us to watch this because we know most of your companies know what to do to make sure they don't fall into this deep, dark hole. In fact, we have taught many people how to do this effectively both for the short-term and the long-term benefit of their companies.

If you want to know how to do what you are doing without making a monumental, bone-headed mistake, call us. We promise we can help you do it effectively without hurting the spirit of human beings you employ.

You and your company get to choose between being humane and being inhumane. It's clearly in your court.

Feedback on: "Employer Retaliation and Other Stupid Mistakes"

WMF® Graduates Newsletter December 2009

Susan and John,

The article in the newsletter about employee retaliation is great.

I saw many managers starting this with companies I worked for. So sad to see many employees having phony performance reviews given to them.

My manager at one company tried to do that to me (my clue that the ax was coming) and I wrote a rebuttal letter, with the facts. The company lawyers had a field day with this guy. He was let go. The key is this, keep things documented always. Have witnesses and keep logs. So sad you have to do that these days. Nice to work for a small company that doesn't do that crap. We have other crap, but not that kind.

A WMF® graduate

This really hit home for me. As a victim first and a survivor next, I was the employee who suddenly was performing far below standards, I was placed on a performance improvement plan after ten-plus years as an exceeds-performer. Suddenly nothing

I did was correct and the emotional abuse was horrific.

Thankfully I am a graduate of 'Women Moving Forward®' which gave me the courage to say *no* to letting the company treat me that way and impact my emotional well-being and self-confidence. That doesn't mean it wasn't a very long, hard road, but I kept my head up and knew that I was not the slacker I was being accused of being.

This kind of activity from employers is far more prevalent than many realize. It's also the most disrespectful behavior I have ever encountered. How can it be more acceptable to treat a long-term employee in this manner than to have a face-to-face discussion where you tell them 'its time to do something else or go somewhere else and then take time to help them move on.

I truly don't know what the resolution for this is, but clearly the current direction is not appropriate. For me, it took an attorney and eight months to work through. But I was steadfast in my determination that I wasn't leaving with that kind of negative mark on my career. *Don't* back down.

A WMF® graduate

Gossip
WMF® Graduates Newsletter March 2010

Across the globe I meet women whose reputations have been forever ruined by negative gossip. Some have been fired and others demoted on the basis of stupid comments that found their way around their companies or communities.

Let's first be clear on what we mean by *gossip*. The dictionary definition is interesting: "rumor or report of an intimate nature." Negative gossip would simply be a negative rumor or a negative report of an intimate nature.

Anthropologists and sociologists will tell you that gossip is an important part of the ethnography of a particular culture. That means gossip is often controlled by the culture in which the gossip is traded.

I am most concerned, where women are concerned, about the use of negative gossip to ruin another woman's reputation as well as the lack of support from other women in the culture. We need to intervene when a woman is clearly being hurt by unsubstantiated negative gossip.

This year alone, in the last two months, I have collected data that shows that ten women were, for lack of a better description, *trashed* by fellow women for no good reason.

None of these women were first approached to check out the validity of the negative gossip and none were confronted directly by the person who started the negative gossip against them.

Understand that I am not talking about substantiated behavior. I am talking about negative gossip like,

- "She had an affair with him you know."
- "She just doesn't do her job."
- "She's too aggressive."
- "She and her husband don't get along."
- "She's crazy because she expects us to follow *all* the regulations."

Some of these comments are the kind of comments we make all day long about other women. Some are subtle, but some are flat-out attacks.

We need to be more thoughtful in our speech when we are addressing the reputations of our sisters. Do we want to continue to establish a culture in which anyone can say anything about a woman and it is used against her for her lifetime in that culture?

As some of you know I have personally been the target of this kind of negative gossip in my own family. It has now gone through three generations of my family and seems to have a life of it's own with the third generation, who weren't even alive at the time of the incidents they are speaking about.

If your answer is no, you don't want to gossip about other women (and it should be no, given you could be the beneficiary of this slander at some point), then I recommend you implement the following steps:

1. Stop trading in negative gossip when talking about your fellow women, especially if it is unsubstantiated and you are passing it on without any personal experience with it.

2. When you hear negative gossip ask the person delivering it if she has evidence that this is true. If the answer is "no",

and it usually is, let her know you are not available to hear it and you will not pass it along.

If you just do these two actions you, will significantly reduce gossip and it's effect on the women in your circle, including you.

Feedback on: "Gossip"
WMF® Graduates Newsletter April 2010

Susan,

Your article on gossip was great. One thing I would like to add, which I learned as I watched one woman in my former company "pick off" the other women in the company through her gossip, is that not participating is not enough. Despite the fact that she had the owner's ear at all times, if we had banded together as a group and met with upper management, we could have at least shown our solidarity as women and been more formidable as such. As it was, we either left of our own accord or became her next victim.

Absolutely feel free to use these comments. Believe me, I wish I had done more than remain silent. She did some real damage to people I worked with and cared about. One girl still can't get a job in professional sports because the woman told everyone that she slept with a player from another team (we worked for a professional hockey team). It didn't happen, but it didn't matter. Damage done, it went national.

A WMF® graduate

Hi, Susan,

I can appreciate your comments regarding negative gossip. This can be so insidious in our culture; it's worse inside corporate than out, but still not good. I've also found that perpetuating the positive can be contagious within a network of friends, once the members pick up that this is the expected behavior and when harmful comments are met with silence.

Love to you and your family and our extended Women Moving Forward® family around the world.

A WMF® graduate

I am so glad that you wrote about gossip in your newsletter this month.

Before I left one company and while at another, I experienced this as a growing issue at both places. It was becoming an accepted practice in the culture, and was part of belonging to the "in club."

It totally amazed me how careless women were in disparaging their sisters, without any data to support their comments as well as not even confronting the person to verify if there were any facts to substantiate the comments.

This has been escalating and becoming a more accepted practice, and I find it totally bewildering. I have found many men participating in this practice too. Luckily at my small company, this behavior is not out there as a culture the "club" accepts.

A WMF® graduate

The message you have on gossip that harms women is so pertinent. I will use it in my class of Business Communication when I teach Grapevine.

May you have a long and healthy life and all the happiness in this world.

My fingers are crossed today as the Women's Reservation Bill is being tabled, if it gets approved, then women will get 33 percent representation in the Assembly. Political empowerment is very important in my opinion.

A WMF® graduate
India

Is Your Company a Tease?
WMF® Graduates Newsletter October 2010

When I was a young woman attending High School in Trenton,

New Jersey, a girl who flirted with boys but did not "put out" (have sex) were "a tease."

I'm sure there are new terms now and, I'm just as sure there are terms men have in every language for girls like this.

That's not the point of this article. The point is I think some of your companies flirt with you and don't "put out" and therefore deserve the label "tease."

A company that is a tease promises you if you do what you are told to do, get the numbers they want you to get, and work very hard, you will be promoted. Somehow I think the boys I knew in high school would call that as much of a tease as many of us were.

The problem with this is you never get what was promised. You never get the new assignment, you never get the promotion and you never get to feel better about yourself because you were worthy enough in their eyes for them to give you what you asked for.

For young men in high school the feeling they get from teases is primarily confusion. They feel they are getting double messages, she likes me enough to treat me this way but doesn't like me enough to have sex with me.

Isn't that what some of you are left with? It's the feeling that they trust you to do lots for the company and to rate you pretty well in performance appraisals, but nothing ever comes of it and you feel confused.

So many of your calls to us are about helping to translate what your company has just said to you. Often we can translate it, but just as often we can't even decipher what they are talking about.

Men go through this too, but they are much better at hearing the real message and, more importantly, at not taking it personally.

We hear the "tease" and the subsequent lack of "put out" as a personal statement of who and what we are.

None of the boys I knew took it personally when a tease didn't "put out."

They moved on to the next girl. Even if they did take it personally for a while, they didn't do it long term. If they had, none of them would have dated at all.

If there is one thing I can advise you to do it's don't believe "the tease" and don't take it personally when your company doesn't "put out." That is the worst thing you can do!

So next time you call having been "corporately teased" with no "put out" I will remind you it has nothing to do with you and everything to do with them and their latest attempt to manipulate you.

Call if you need to have this conversation.

And, let us know if you have an example of this in your own life. We always value your responses.

Feedback on: "Is Your Company a Tease?"
WMF® Graduates Newsletter November 2010

Susan,

Your tease article was so good this month. We have all been teased for years with the big guys. I used to call it the never-ending carrot dangle. (amazing metaphor, LOL!)

What is even sadder, is to see other women become the surrogate of these teasing messages. The betrayal that one feels from the other women, goes right along with that.

I think it is so important as you mention to make sure that you don't tell yourself any stories of not being good enough or not being valuable enough. This is how we get caught in the trap of wanting outside approval. We all need validation at times, but it needs to come from trustworthy people, people we know who can honestly evaluate how we have done our jobs.

Too many corporate performance appraisals these days have become weapons held for future potential lawsuits, not honest performance evaluations. That is why keeping trustworthy people on hand to give us honest feedback is so important for validating ourselves. That is probably the most helpful thing we can do for other women, IMHO.

My own way of keeping my self-esteem in-tact, is to remind myself when these mixed massages show up, that I and my work have integrity. (I am also careful not to put perfectionist standards on myself here) And I have character in how I do my business dealings. I always like to remind other women who come to me when these teases show up. I refuse to give my personal power away to some bozo trying to get his ego pumped up. They only have power over me when I give mine away to them. The grandest way to keep my power is to value who I am every single day when I wake up in the morning.

A WMF® graduate

Age Bias and Gender Bias
WMF® Graduates Newsletter December 2010

For the last few months I have been following two lawsuits: the Google age-discrimination lawsuit and the Wal-Mart gender-bias lawsuit.

The former was already ruled on by the State of California Supreme Court: It should proceed to trial, and the latter will be in the Supreme Court of the United States very soon, because the highest court agreed to hear it.

These cases if won by the folks who have brought them, could make legal history in the United States. The Wal-mart suit could be the largest in US history just by the sheer number of women involved in the suit.

The suits interest me, but I'm no lawyer. What interests me is the level of arrogance exhibited by both of these companies that led them to this special place in legal history.

What I mean by *arrogance* is the fact that both had previous warnings that they were discriminating (Wal-mart had previous suits) and yet they felt they were above the law or, more importantly above the morality that not discriminating demands.

For me, this is an issue of immorality.

When you discriminate against a whole group of humans and then continue to do so even when asked to correct your behavior, you are immoral, that is, you are purposely going against moral values.

Also, when you ignore these values and do whatever you want and when you tolerate your employees and management doing the same you are immoral.

We are entering into a time of year when people celebrating very important holidays with deep religious messages.

Can we call for a higher moral bar for companies when it comes to discrimination? Can we also expect our own companies and organizations to live up to those standards?

Pat Bowlen, the owner of the Denver Broncos football team, recently fired the head coach because he violated Pat's high moral standards. This is a standard I wish all companies had.

Pat felt he had worked long and hard to establish a moral bar for owners of professional teams and in fact he had. He is considered one of the best owners in the United States.

Here's what appears to be Pat's standard: don't accept Immoral behavior of any kind as normal even from your team's head coach.

If you have employees or managers who continually discriminate, and you have tried to correct them or retain them but they have not changed, you need to fire them. Their behavior is immoral and you can't afford to be seen as an immoral company.

Thanks, Pat, for showing us how high we need to hold the bar.

Could Watson, the IBM Super Computer Lead Women Moving Forward?

WMF® Graduates Newsletter March 2011

For the last week an IBM super computer, Watson, has appeared on *Jeopardy* and beat two humans at the game. The conversation that has transpired on every US TV show has been about whether computers can replace all of us in our jobs.

I think this whole conversation is ridiculous at best. (Sometimes I wonder if the press just likes to scare us senseless for no good reason.) That's not to say that I believe there will not be some jobs that computers, especially of the Watson variety, will take for humans.

So I decided to apply this concept of computers taking over our jobs to my own job. More specifically, could a computer lead Women Moving Forward®?

Well, as I looked at the different sections of the course; Introduction, Culture, Perfection, Balance, Suppression and Denial Bridge, Completion Exercise, and so on. I found there were some sections I'll bet Lorrie and I would be happy to let Watson do!

But unless Watson can duplicate the nuances in our voices and read the thoughts in women's eyes, I'm not sure our jobs are in jeopardy quite yet.

I think we have plenty of workshops to lead in our future.

Some of you, have already seen layoffs from increased use of computer systems and automation, so we want to know what you think and feel about this topic.

- What do you think will happen in your role in twenty years?

- What has already changed in the last five years?

- What roles do you think are most in jeopardy?

Male Chauvinist Pigs, or *Les Phallocrate*
WMF® Graduates Newsletter June 2011

In the sixties those of us in the women's movement called them MCPs, or male chauvinist pigs.

I just saw the latest issue of *Time* in which the pig moniker was being dusted off and used on the cover of the magazine. It's about time.

When my son Charlie was about four or five, I taught him how to shoot a basketball in our driveway. He would try and then I would shoot one and score a basket.

He got so frustrated he said he wanted to wait for Daddy to come home to play.

I looked at him and said, "You're a little, male chauvinist pig!" He said, "I'm no pig!" I'm not sure he knew what that was, but he sure knew it wasn't a good thing. Well, maybe Charlie isn't a pig, but the news worldwide is full of them. Dominique Strauss-Kahn, John Edwards and Arnold Schwarzenegger, to name a few, have been in the news lately.

Women all over the world are reassessing what sexual harassment is and where the line is crossed to assault. That's the good news! But women are also asking what produces this behavior in men and what can we do to eradicate it?

My first answer is they are mentally ill. Maybe I answered that way because I just spent two days at the women's leadership retreat describing mental illnesses in the workplace. Or, maybe it's just my social work mind-set, which would say, they are mentally ill.

116

They have a form of mental illness that manifests itself in this type of behavior toward women. I hesitate to diagnose each of these men, but clearly they were all warned and still participated in what can best be described as self-defeating behaviors. All seem to feel an entitlement and an invincibility that comes with several mental illnesses.

In some ways, our society in some ways encourages this behavior. We make excuses for men like this as if what's between their legs determines this behavior, when it is really what's between their ears.

I have often said that when women get sick of being sexually harassed at work the sexual harassment stops. I'm not blaming the victim; I'm simply saying that we women need to raise our consciousness to tell the truth about what is really going on.

When we as women use the phrases;

- "Men will be men."
- "It's just the usual male/female issues."
- "They just don't understand what they are doing."

we become part of the problem, which means we cannot be the solution.

This is why training like Women Moving Forward® which brings women together so they can actually talk about it, is so important. The real message is that we don't tolerate piggish behavior from men. Whenever we do, we send them a message that they can get away with it. The best way to deal with this is to confront the situation as a group and demand a change.

If men you know continue in the same bad behavior no matter what intervention is tried, they need to be let go or sent to therapy. Nothing less is acceptable because your workplace and home need to be safe for you.

Nothing stops this behavior faster then a firing. Men who are pigs respond faster than a New York minute when they see a fellow pig let go. They get religion. And, in one case we were involved in, they become paragons of a harassment-free workplace.

And while we are discussing this, kudos to the maid at the Sofitel Hotel in New York! She is my hero.

Guess What? Women are Valuable on a Team
WMF® Graduates Newsletter 2012

Who would have thought it?

Two researchers, Anita Woolley and Thomas Malone, reported in the June 2011 HBR that the only variable that predicted the success of a team was the inclusion of women.

That's right. Purely the inclusion of us makes a team more successful. They studied other variables like the collective intelligence of team members and the only variable that made a difference, according to their research, was the presence of women on the team.

Now, some of us already knew this, but it is nice to hear it backed up by research.

What we already knew is women bring the special ability to use influencing skills like listening to the whole group. Apparently the special skills women come to the table with are the very skills that make a team a success.

I have two suggestions:

1. Get a copy of the study and paper your entire company with it.

2. Do not give up the skills you, as a woman, bring to the table in order to look more like the male power holders around you.

For those of you needing rehab in the skills you used to have I recommend our Productive Relationships© workshop. It will give you a good refresher of the skills the researchers say we have and need for successful teams.

Congratulations women, our skills have finally been proven to be needed for success.

Let us know what you think and how your skills have made teams you have been in successful.

WOMEN MOVING FORWARD®
CHAPTER 10
DIVERSITY

- On Behalf of Women Everywhere
- Hello

On Behalf of Women Everywhere
WMF® Graduates Newsletter October 2005

After traveling in Europe, Asia and South America the last two years it has become abundantly clear to me that women are women wherever we are from. We have the same struggles some of us just have more dire punishments for not fitting the norm. If my observations are correct and you agree that we are the same across political, cultural, religious and ethnic boundaries then as women we cannot afford to be xenophobic in our working together.

If my hypothesis is correct we must work to banish from our thoughts and speaking any territorial prejudices and replace them with acceptance and a renewed focus on these issues:

- Create more viable support systems for woman globally. For example, women need to have a safe place to live and an abundance of clean water and food to sustain themselves and their children.

- Banish all abuse of women globally, no matter what the excuse or what the rationale.

- Make high-quality education available to all women and girls.

These three are just the beginning. They will be followed by more complicated ways to support all women everywhere, but at least we can start with these.

So if you find yourself talking about someone and using a racial, territorial, or ethnic slur stop and find some other way to express your self-prejudice free. We are all in this together and we cannot use our old prejudices to band together and make the three issues I described above a reality. From this point on you may be from the United States but you are a woman of the world, supporting all women everywhere. You may be from Argentina but you are also working for women in China; you may be from Japan, but you are also ready to stand with women from Chile.

If we don't do this, we will be part of the problem, not the solution.

If you are ready to stand with me on this and accept my challenge let me know. Let me know what you plan to do to act, or what you are already doing. It doesn't have to be big; it can be you watching what you say to make sure it is prejudice-free.

If you cannot accept my challenge, I understand. Take some time to think about it. You may not be ready now, but may be later.

Hello

We are straying from our usual WMF® Newsletter Format for August and we are asking you to read the latest issue of the "online" Diversity Inc. newsletter. You can access it through: http://www.diversityinc.com

The article is entitled: Why Aren't More Black Women Getting Promoted?

It talks about the junctures at which Black Women get discriminated against and what pressures are on them to conform. It also talks about the need for Black Women to Network in order to manage their careers.

I know some of you come from countries in which race may not be an issue in Diversity as it is in the US. For those of you for whom this is true look at this article from the point of view of whatever group of women is discriminated against in your culture, country or company. Are the pressures for those women the same as for Black Women here? What do they need to do in your country or culture to get ahead?

After you read the article let me know what you think. Is it applicable in your life and if so how? How do you see it working where you live and work? I want to hear from you about this.

WOMEN MOVING FORWARD®
CHAPTER 11
MENTAL HEALTH

- Emotional Abuse – Silent Voices

- Not Guilty by Reason of Insanity

- Women, Stay Sane if You Can

- Feedback on: "Stay Sane if You Can"

Emotional Abuse – Silent Voices
October 2001

Emotional abuse is a category of abuse no one wants to discuss. It affects the nature of the whole relationship a woman has with a partner. It is not overt like physical abuse, so it is harder to detect and treat.

However, it is the most devastating form of abuse because it attacks you at the core of your self-esteem. Some victims of emotional abuse don't even know it is going on.

I have seen very successful professional women suffer from emotional abuse at the hands of parents, partners and husbands. Vice-presidents, directors, CEOs, none of these categories are exempt from emotional abuse.

At work, these women can command large salaries and bonuses. They may manage millions of dollars in corporate budgets and thousands of people. But at home they feel dumb, incompetent and unsuccessful, because someone is there to make sure they feel like that all the time.

The very nature of emotional abuse is a slow, chipping away of a women's self-esteem and confidence. If you get told you are not good enough long enough, you start to believe it. The abuser knows this and artfully orchestrates the abuse so you may not even recognize it is going on.

I've seen many forms of emotional abuse. Here are some examples:

1. You are told repeatedly (either in words or by actions) that you are a loser, worthless, or incompetent in some way, or

in every way. This is usually around the children or some other home situation. The abuser makes you feel as if you are to blame for any and all problems in the relationship.

2. Your spouse or partner forms a close relationship with your children or friends, parents, and so on. Your spouse or partner uses these relationships to put you down and discredit you. You find yourself less and less in relationship with these folks.

3. You treat the abuser with kid gloves. You walk on eggshells and make sure the abuser is never upset. You prepare others to do the same, or you never allow others to be around you and the abuser.

4. You know the abuser is having an affair; you have evidence that he/she is. He/She might even wave it in your face as if to say you are worthless. When you confront your abuser, he/she denies the affair and tries to make you feel crazy for bringing it up.

5. They never support any ideas, directions, actions or new challenges you want to take on. Sometimes they passive-aggressively go along and then sabotage it. The finally seal the abuse with comments like "See, you said you wanted to do it and now look at what happened!" or "How can you spend so much time away from your family, we need you here."

6. You are completely financially and emotionally responsible for the entire family and the abuser still objects to you spending money or making decisions for the family. Your abuser may try to control you through the finances of the family.

If any of these examples ring true for you, you will need to take some action.

First, get yourself into therapy and identify why you accept this kind of abuse. Begin to set boundaries for the abuser with your therapist's help. You can also set the boundary of them going into therapy as well.

Second, if the abuser continues the abuse or it escalates into physical abuse, you must make some important decisions and take action. You may have to leave him/her. I warn you that without some intervention, it will only get worse. Moreover, if there are children, you are modeling the acceptance of emotional abuse as part of a relationship.

If you find after reading this you are a part of an emotionally abusive relationship, call us. We will assist you in finding support where you are.

But, be forewarned: we will not support you in staying in an emotionally abusive relationship; we will only support you in getting help.

Not Guilty by Reason of Insanity
WMF® Graduates Newsletter August 2006

For those of you who don't know, Andrea Yates, who killed her children in a bathtub several years ago, was sentenced to life imprisonment, had a second trial and was found guilty by reason of insanity. For John and me, and all social service people we know, this was quite a victory. It means even your average jury in Texas can understand the subtle nuances of what a mental illness is.

Her history was the definition of insanity. Andrea had a severe mental illness for which she had been hospitalized several times. Her mental illness was exasperated by a very severe form of postpartum depression called postpartum psychosis. She heard voices, visually hallucinated and generally was not emotionally available for over five years before the incident.

She continued to have children after her first bout of postpartum psychosis, even though the psychiatrist at the mental hospital told her and her husband not to have any more children (they had three at the time) and to keep her on medication at all costs. She went to another doctor, who took her off her medication – the only thing keeping her somewhat sane – so she could get pregnant again, which was what her husband wanted.

Her husband had made arrangements for his mother to watch the children when he wasn't there, since even he noticed she wasn't capable anymore. But on the day of the incident, he left her alone with the children for two hours so he could be on time for work.

So, what does this verdict mean and why are all of us in the mental health field happy?

First, it means maybe, just maybe, there will be more understanding for those with mental illnesses. Maybe other people will submit to quality treatment without being afraid of being locked up.

Second, it means women with Postpartum Depression will be seen as having a *real* mental illness, not just a made-up or fake one. It also means people get it that there are gradations of mental illness and Andrea Yates had one of the most severe.

Third, we hope people get it – You can't ignore someone this mentally ill. It won't go away with love and rest. It's a condition as real as cancer that needs to be treated as seriously as cancer. By the way, it isn't confined to just the community you live in, it shows up at work too!

Fourth, as Andrea's lawyer so eloquently put it, "Kids deserve to have parents as free from mental illness as possible." I've been waiting a long time to hear someone say that in public. Kids deserve to have parents who are as sane as possible, or we doom the next generation to mental illness as well.

Graduates of WMF know how important sane parenting was, or could have been, for them. You may know what having mentally ill parents did to you and how it follows you into adulthood and to work.

Fifth, we hope Andrea's story makes you demand the quality of mental health care you deserve and your family deserves, regardless of what country or city you live in or what company you work for.

Start forcing your governments and companies to allocate money for high-quality mental health care.

And, remember, children deserve the most mentally healthy parents they can have. Make sure you remember that, and maybe, just maybe we can prevent another tragedy.

Women, Stay Sane If You Can
WMF® Graduates Newsletter June 2012

In the last few months I have had the privilege to talk to so many of you from all over the world and one thing is true across the board: your companies are just trying to survive, and therefore not acting normally.

Yes, companies can be abnormal and crazy as entities. The culture in many companies today is one of neurosis, if not psychosis.

That means the culture is crazy and so it becomes even more important for you to stay sane during this very crazy period in your company.

So, this means, if you stay sane, you will be running counter to the culture in which you work every day. This is no easy feat! To stay sane when the culture around you is crazy takes a lot of work.

You may ask, "What do I need to do to stay sane when everyone around me is crazy?" I thought you might ask, so here are some steps to take to remain sane:

1. Beef up your support system outside of the company and make sure you have people to see and things to do *outside* your company.

   In this situation it is critical to keep the distinction between your personal and work life. You must have people to talk to who *are not* with your company.

2. This is the time to do something you've wanted to do but haven't had the time. Start cooking classes, dancing

classes, or do something else you've put on the back burner. Yes, this will require time and effort but it will also give you with time away from the crazy culture in your office.

3. You must limit the time you spend in the crazy culture. Even trained therapists do this with clients and institutions. None of them spend the hours you do at work and therefore are immersed all day in insanity. Get out any way you can. Work from home, travel, or take meetings somewhere other than the office. Do not stay immersed in this kind of culture the way you did before.

4. Double the time you take to relax. If you don't do anything now, start. It is imperative that you learn to relax and take the time to do so.

5. Get professional help if you need it! At least have the name of someone on speed dial. Therapists always have other therapists to go to for support. We never work alone on craziness. You will need to deal with some things you are not prepared to handle; that's when a professional needs to handle it. Make sure you also have a beefed-up EAP service and that you know how to make referrals to it.

I know what I am telling you is the antithesis of what you may believe you need to do in this crazy culture, but the counter-intuitive nature of it will keep you sane while dealing with insanity all around you.

Feedback on: "Women, Stay Sane If You Can"
WMF® Graduates Newsletter July 2012

Apparently this article hit a nerve with a lot of readers and I hope you are learning from the feedback we reprint.

Let us know if we can help you as you navigate the changes you are dealing with.

> Susan,
>
> I hope all is well with you and John,
>
> I am writing you a short note to say thank you for "Women, Stay Sane If You Can." Your advice really works and I forwarded it to some other women. Generally I noticed that WMF graduates are dealing with the change better than the rest of the community.
>
> I turned my office into an "isle of sanity" and refused to be driven into the overall madness despite a difficult job situation. Needless to say, the people in charge of this mess are men. I clearly communicated to my management that I see it as their job to solve the problem, not mine. And I manage to stay cool by following your sanity tips, including yoga, home office day and a weekly movie night out with my husband.
>
> Ironically, my team loves me at the moment probably because I am more relaxed. The only pity is that I had to put my sabbatical plans on hold for

the time being as I decided that it is not very wise to disappear from the radar screen right now.

Best regards,
A WMF® graduate

WOMEN MOVING FORWARD®
CHAPTER 12
DECISIONS AND CHOICES

- Women, Don't Give Up Your Power

- WMF® Graduate Reply

- Perfectionism Will Kill You

- On Becoming the Woman You Are

- Responsibility

- Feedback on: "Responsibility"

Women Don't Give Up Your Power
WMF® Graduates Newsletter February 2006

Recently I tuned into the current season of *The Bachelor* on TV. Maybe I was bored or maybe I needed to be awakened to the fact that the current crop of young women is as needy and messed up as we all were. All I know is that I am now convinced that we have a lot of work to do.

First of all, no normal, healthy woman *needs* a man to survive. We may want to be with a man or work for a man, but that's not the same as *needing* one to be complete or to survive. The bad news is, if you feel you *need* a man to survive, you need help. This is not a joke; it's serious. You need help. Let us know if you want a referral to a therapist.

Make no mistake: I want to be with John, I love John, I chose to be with John and everyday I take responsibility for that choice. However, it is also true I don't, nor have I ever, *needed* to be with him. That, by the way, is one of the reasons I married him. I didn't need him and he didn't need me to need him.

And that's my second point: if a man *needs* you to *need* him, you're with a guy who needs constant reassurance that he is a man. A real man doesn't need you to need him. He wants a partner in life, not a dependent.

Thirdly, if you have a relationship with a man in a prominent position, such as a doctor or president of a corporation, you will work harder to meet his needs than you would if he were an ordinary "Joe Shmoe." This season's bachelor is an emergency room doctor. I can't even imagine what you would have to do to keep a family going if your husband was an emergency room doctor.

Okay, that's my rant for this month. What do you think?

WMF Graduate Reply
WMF® Graduates Newsletter May 2006

I received this email from a graduate of WMF® last month and I asked her if I could share it with you. I thought hearing about her journey might benefit some of you who are struggling with the same issues.

Susan,

I am unsure you will remember me. I am one of the surely many, many women you have helped over the years. My former boss knew I would benefit from your Women Moving Forward® class a few years back. Well, I want to proudly say that I am in the middle of my long overdue divorce!

I had shared with you and the other women in our Women Moving Forward® class that I was in a verbally abusive relationship and wanted to "fix" it for the wellbeing of all involved, my husband, my two girls and me. Finally, after years of trying (sixteen different counseling attempts) as well as getting the push from you through your course, I finally got the nerve, spirit and power to move on with my life.

My girls (Hannah, 17 and Emma, 14) asked, "Mom, why did you wait so long?" I now know, looking back, that I really should have made this move years ago. Anyway, I am now enthusiastically looking forward to the future, with or without a man, knowing I am facing much brighter, happier and healthier days to come!

I just wanted to tell you that I appreciate you, your wisdom, and your courage and I am glad we crossed paths when we did, for surely I, my girls and even my ex-husband will be better for it. Thank you from the bottom of my heart for all you did for me and for the many other women that need to face the facts and *just move forward!*

Lots of love,
A WMF® Graduate

Remember, you must listen to your own time clock on issues like this and make decisions that work for you. She made the right decision at the right time for hers and that is what is so important about her journey in addition to her realizing the toll the verbal and emotional abuse had taken on her and her family.

Thank you to this graduate for sharing her story with all of us and for making a difference by letting us use her story to support other women.

Perfectionism Will Kill You
WMF® Graduates Newsletter February 2007

Lately, I've seen a lot of women suffering from the expectations they put on themselves, expectations of perfectionism in all areas of their life. At age sixty, I can look back to a time in my life when I did that too, but I was never as ruthless with myself as some of you appear to be with yourselves.

"You are your own worst enemy" is a phrase I find myself using more and more when I speak with women.

"Be the best person you can be" has been over shadowed by: "Have a perfect body, hair, clothes, car and place to live. Also be the perfect employee, mother, wife and partner." If it stopped with you, I would say, "Okay, go ahead and try." but you might also be placing these expectations on your kids and on people you live with and work with. That is not just being obsessive-compulsive yourself, but also making everyone else responsible for your mental illness.

Perfection is not a goal but an obsession. It's a mental illness of sorts because there is no such thing as perfection in anything. So it is a fantasy you judge yourself against and you always come up short or lacking. It is a place you go when you want to punish yourself. In fact, traditional Japanese artists purposely include an imperfection in their work so they do not risk making a "perfect piece of artwork."

Here are some suggestions to rehabilitate yourself from perfectionism.

1. Start small. Let something be imperfect, in fact, leave it undone. I always suggest starting with something small, like your bathroom shower.

140

2. Write a full description of what your life would be like and look like if it were perfect. Don't forget to include a description of you. Take the time to do it fully, the more detail the better. When you finish, check your description against reality. Is it possible or is it just a cartoonish description that no one can match?

3. If you cannot get yourself out of this paradigm you may need to get help. Join a support group to check out reality, or go to a therapist.

Trust me. This perfection paradigm will kill you, especially as you age. If you think you're imperfect now, just wait until you turn sixty.

On Becoming the Woman You Are
WMF® Graduates Newsletter September 2007

As I was watching the movie; *Becoming Jane* about the British author, Jane Austin, I was thinking about all the ways I and women
like me have had to work outside the cultures in which we were
raised to live the life we choose.

Austin was considered an early feminist writer because in all of
her books her heroines are very independent and intelligent for
the age and time in which she wrote.

At her time women were not allowed to inherit; only men received
inheritances. Women of her age were not allowed to make their
own livings; their husbands and fathers did that. So a woman
who was not married, had no children, and had a career, like
writing, was considered odd and weird. She and her family were
ostracized.

Austin had to operate outside the norm of her culture to be a
successful writer. Many of us have to do the same thing as she
did; we have to operate in the culture we are from, not having the
"normal" behavior of women in our culture.

We choose to do that for ourselves so that we can create the life
we want to live. We do it to have the life that is best for us. We
find the guts and courage to tell family and friends, clergy and
teachers, that we are going to live a different life from the one they
want us to live or the life they had to live.

For some of you, as for me, this decision, even in the twenty-first
century, has made you a stranger or a freak in your own culture.
When we choose to live our life as we feel best, we face what

Susan Faludi referred to in her book as "backlash", and she used the term as the book's title.

The culture and some individuals in it will attack us for our choices. Sometimes it is a subtle response to something we said. It says, "I disapprove of what you chose to do". Other times it is a full-out,direct assault on what we hold most dear.

To combat the societal backlash, or to support your life choices you need increased support from women who are going through the same thing or support from older women who have come through to the other side of what you are struggling with now.

Part of the importance of Women Moving Forward® and the Women's Leadership Retreat©, is they are places to receive and give this kind of support to each other.

These workshops are places for you to support each other in a similar stand to the one Austin took for herself: the desire to have a life you can look back on with pride in your accomplishments both personally and professionally.

I can tell you it is not an easy way to live your life but it is *very satisfying.*

Let me know what you have done and how you have done it to be successful against the odds of the culture in which you were raised and what support you have had to do it successfully.

Responsibility
WMF® Graduates Newsletter August 2011

I know that experiences in Women Moving Forward® are ones of self-discovery and dropping old baggage so you can move on with your life.

Women Moving Forward® is also about taking responsibility for your life and moving forward.

This is not always easy, as you can attest. In some ways, it is easier to not take responsibility and to blame your condition on your family, company, and so on. Sometimes it looks easier not to be responsible.

Responsibility for your life is hard, because it means you have to always be honest with yourself about who is in charge. You can't ever defer to someone else for your wellbeing.

It is always fun to see the new participants on day 1 of the workshop struggling with this concept. In fact WMF® participants struggle with responsibility long before the first day of the workshop.

All of the pre-work starts the ball rolling, forcing women across the world to look at who is in charge and why. As you may know, the reaction of some women to the pre-work is fear. That is, they appear to be afraid of the gravity of the questions on the pre-work.

Actually, what many of them are afraid of or angry about is the responsibility they are forced to take for their lives just by filling out the pre-work. Some are so clear they do not want to take responsibility, they drop out when they see the pre-work.

I know I have said, "Please let them drop out angry at me and the workshop. Don't force them to see the light. They need to have an out, especially if they are clear they are not willing to take responsibility at that level."

For those of you who work with or live with women and men who won't take responsibility, I'm sorry to say you don't have a lot of options.

You must somehow make them overtly responsible for something and stop propping them up. If you continue to prop them up, you continue to make them co-dependent on you. That means they make you responsible for them for the rest of your life.

In other words, take the lessons you learn from Women Moving Forward® and apply them to those folks.

Feedback on: "Responsibility"
WMF® Graduates Newsletter September 2011

The article on responsibility reminded me of something John wisely told me when we faced trying to locate jobs within our organization for team members whose positions were being eliminated. John's advice was, "You can't be more committed to your people than they are to themselves. If you are, they'll *get* you for it."

I've been reminded of that quite often over the last seven years at work and in my personal life. Taking responsibility for myself and allowing others to take responsibility for themselves is a skill I continue to practice; I wish I could say I was 100 percent successful.

A WMF® graduate

WOMEN MOVING FORWARD®
CHAPTER 13
AGING

On Becoming Gray
WMF® Graduates Newsletter April 2002

Many of you haven't seen me since you attended Women Moving Forward®. Just in case we meet again soon let me tell you I've changed.

First, I'm fifty-five years old, menopausal and I've decided to let my hair go to it's natural color: gray.

I did not decide to go gray because I can't afford to dye it every 4 weeks or because it takes an extra hour and a half every four weeks to do it. Even though those are great reasons, my reason was more of an internal statement; I don't want to be something I'm not and it irks me and makes me uncomfortable when I'm not congruent. I don't expect my life to change drastically because I'm no longer dying my hair, but I already feel better about me.

As my children grow up and leave home and as I change my definition of me, for the next part of life, my gray hair is outward manifestation of my internal theme: *who I am on the outside is who I am on the inside.*

That is just the way it is.

How to Contact Us

Susan Van Vleet Consultants, Inc ® (SVVCI®) works with a diverse group of companies and organizations across the world.

SVVCI® can design programs for your company or organization that meet your immediate and long-term needs.

You can find us through our websites, as well as through LinkedIn and FaceBook.

You can also contact us directly:

Susan Van Vleet Consultants, Inc.
31416 Agoura Rd. Ste 255
Westlake Village, CA. 91361
Phone 303.660.5206
Email svvconsult@svanvleetconsult.com

Websites:

Svanvleetconsult.com and womenmovingforward.com

Our Distributors
Lorrie Teitze
Interface Consulting
lbtietze@interfaceconsultingonline.com

Robin Elston
Elston Consulting, LLC
relston@bright.net

Kate Gruninger Johnson
Gracecamp Consulting
Kate@gracecamp.com